Saint Jerome

By Father Largent

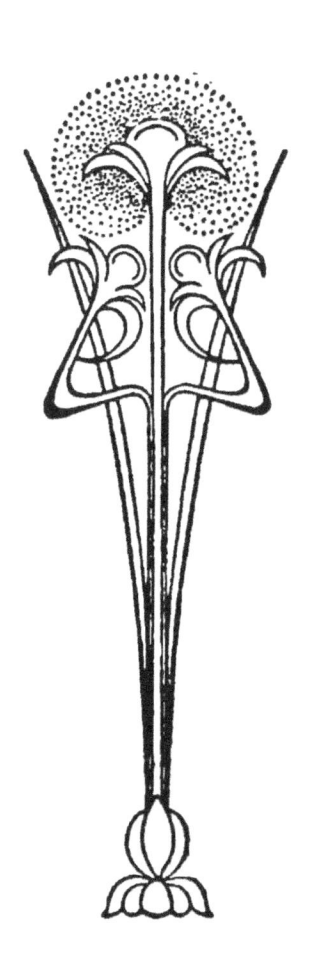

Translated by
Hester Davenport

PREFACE

ST JEROME, though one of the four "great" doctors of the Church, seems never to have been an object of any very tender personal devotion as other saints have been, his appeal being more directly to the head than to the heart. His sanctity and austerity is of the kind that awes rather than attracts, and is provocative of admiration rather than of imitation. For this reason he has been looked at with cool, temperate eyes; and since, moreover, he has so fully written himself down for us, there is little difficulty in discerning the broad outlines of his personality.

A strange, strong man, strenuous and intense even to the verge of ferocity, as was the fashion of his day with the champions of orthodoxy; nor is the fashion yet wholly obsolete, for all our longer study of the meekness of Christ. In him is exemplified the sort of antagonism that exists between delicacy of perception and strength of execution, and renders their equal development so rare in one and the same character. With great capacity in both directions, St Jerome seems alternately to sacrifice one of these interests to the other. In his zealous self-hatred it never occurred to him apparently that the difficulties he was contending with were more probably the effect of mental strain and nervous exhaustion than of an overplus of animal energy, and therefore were rather augmented than alleviated by his violent methods. In the feverish vision of his judgment before Christ's tribunal—embodying no doubt the state of his conscience at the time—the whole apparatus of secular learning by which he himself was subsequently enabled to become so acute an exponent and defender of the faith, and which the later Church blessed, sanctified, and consecrated to the service of religion, was condemned without qualification as repugnant to Christianity; even as the body and all natural affections were indiscriminately condemned as inimical to virtue and sanctity.

It is mainly to the gigantic force of his intellect, to his stupendous power of work, to his prodigious scholarship—as scholarship went in those days—that he owes his prominence in the history of Christianity. When we think of what he did, and did single-handed, for scriptural criticism and exegesis: how he created order and coherence where previously there had been wild chaos and confusion; how he expanded and applied the critical principles then in vogue as far as the material to hand would permit; we cannot help wondering what he would do, what he would be allowed to do, were he among us now, and were he master—as doubtless he would be—of the rich harvest of learning and information that has been accumulating during the intervening centuries. Would he regard his past work as final and irreformable, and view subsequent discoveries

PREFACE

with peevish suspicion; or would he welcome truth fearlessly from whatsoever quarter deriving? And the like doubt arises in regard to another eminent doctor—one who embraced and reconciled to the faith that same philosophy which the sub-apostolic Fathers had anathematised, and this, at a time when Peripateticism was in as little favour with Catholics as perhaps Hegelianism is now. What would he think now, what would he say, what would he do?

Doubtless a twentieth century Jerome or Aquinas would be to our day what he was to his own: he would take and give; he would see much good as well as some evil; much light as well as some darkness; he would delight as much in building up and uniting as rigid formalism does in sundering and destroying.

G. TYRRELL.

CONTENTS

	PAGE
INTRODUCTORY	1

CHAPTER I
| YOUTH | 10 |

CHAPTER II
| THE DESERT OF CHALCIS | 19 |

CHAPTER III
| ROME | 32 |

CHAPTER IV
| BETHLEHEM—YEARS OF PEACE | 45 |

CHAPTER V
| CONTENTIONS—RUFINUS AND ORIGENISM | 56 |

CHAPTER VI
| JOYS AND SORROWS—JEROME AS MENTOR | 85 |

CONTENTS

CHAPTER VII

CONTROVERSY WITH SAINT AUGUSTINE   PAGE 96

CHAPTER VIII

THE LAST YEARS OF SAINT JEROME'S LIFE—HIS LAST ORDEALS   115

THE WORKS AND THE TEACHINGS OF SAINT JEROME

CHAPTER I

THE WORKS OF SAINT JEROME   143

CHAPTER II

THE DOCTRINE OF SAINT JEROME   163

SAINT JEROME

INTRODUCTORY

SAINT JEROME, a contemporary of St Ambrose and of St Augustine, who was his junior and survived him, forms with those two great men the incomparable triumvirate of the Latin Church in the fourth and fifth centuries. The Bishop of Milan, the Counsellor of Valentinian II., the friend of Theodosius—St Ambrose, whose eloquence became at times pathetic and soared to the sublime, and who possessed a rare aptitude for government, was the pioneer of Christian statesmen, while St Augustine is pre-eminently the metaphysician of Christianity; none of his predecessors had made a more searching and comprehensive survey of the synthesis of the dogmas, and no one has bequeathed more ideas to posterity. St Jerome, however, did not resemble either St Ambrose or St Augustine in any of the gifts which distinguished them. If he directed the elect few who intrusted their souls to his care, he never dreamed of extending his authority beyond this limited field. The fierce adversary of Helvidius, Jovinian, Vigilantius, Pelagius, and even of Origen, whom at first he had so much admired,

was of course a theologian, but not after the manner of an Augustine, an Anselm, or a Thomas Aquinas. He faithfully and jealously upheld and defended the Catholic dogma, but he did not try to penetrate into it or to throw any light, of necessity essentially imperfect, upon the mysteries of Christianity. Jerome's immense erudition, his critical and exegetical talents, which he devoted to an indefatigable study of the Scriptures, on which point the most contrary opinions have agreed in praising his pre-eminence, are what distinguished him from amongst all the Latin Fathers. "Although," said Richard Simon, "he borrowed many things from Origen, he was, nevertheless, more learned than he in his knowledge of languages.
The Greek Fathers had this advantage over the Latins, that the books of the New Testament were written in their own tongue; but in this particular Jerome yielded nothing to them, and his knowledge of Hebrew, his mastery of the art of criticism, gave him an advantage which they did not possess."[1] Before the days of Richard Simon, the protestant, Joseph Scaliger, Sixtus of Sienna, that pious and learned Dominican, and still further back the ecclesiastical writers and Fathers had signalised these glorious characteristics of Jerome, and the Church, with an authority which has no precedent, thanks God in the prayers on St Jerome's day for having bestowed upon it in this Saint the most dependable interpreter of the Scriptures: " Deus qui Ecclesiæ tuæ in exponendis sacris Scripturis beatum Hiero-

[1] Critical History of the Leading Commentators of the New Testament. Chapter xv.

nymum Doctorem maximum providere dignatus es. . . ."

Other traits further reveal the originality of this historical figure, who was the most learned of the Latins in his knowledge of classic antiquity as well as in the study of the early history of Christianity and the Bible.

Jerome, the "Ancestor of our great humanists," as M. Henri Goelzer called him, was a writer who throughout his career recalled, and reminded others of the masterpieces he had absorbed in his youth. "Transplanted into Oriental soil," wrote Villemain, "amongst Syrians and Hebrews, the idioms of whose languages he frequently employed when translating the Holy Books, he retained in his own writings the purity of the Latin tongue he had spoken in his youth at Rome."[1] His style not only preserved an elegance forgotten by many of his illustrious contemporaries, but it was also eloquent. St Jerome derived his eloquence from his own soul, in which exalted virtues mingled so strangely with undeniable defects. We must not expect to find in him the serene meekness of Ambrose. Like Augustine, he was capable of the most ardent affection, but he also gave way to passionate anger and resentment, neither of which ever troubled the gentle soul of the son of Monica. Violent invectives, hard and unjustifiable accusations seemed to come naturally to him, and as Lenain de Tillemont (whose unpolished language was sometimes most expressive) wrote: "Whoever had Jerome for an adversary was almost

[1] Picture of Christian eloquence in the fourth century.—St Jerome.

always the very last of men."[1] Notwithstanding these defects of character, notwithstanding the mistakes which they occasioned, in spite of the error in judgment which led Jerome to join Theophilus of Alexandria in a deplorable campaign against St John Chrysostom, the hermit of Bethlehem left in the Church a saintly fame which has descended through fourteen centuries. The memory of his priceless works inspired by his passion for truth, and of the penances with which he reduced his flesh, by ridding his soul of importunate recollections of the past and freeing it from dangerous temptations, explain and justify the cult. "Jerome's preference for a life of solitude and poverty when he might have claimed the support of Damasus and disposed of the wealth of St Marcella and St Paula, and his habit of fleeing from those who would pay him homage, were," says Tillemont, an historian not always to be trusted but with whom we can in this instance thoroughly agree, "acts characteristic of a saint alone." An ignorant and narrow conception might wrongfully confound saintliness with impeccability and incapability of erring. No doubt the Saints (I speak of those whom the Church has declared or recognised to be such) all strove after perfection, and all attained to a certain degree of it, but this does not mean that their first effort was crowned with success. They did not all escape the errors of judgment and conduct which reveal the presence of original sin even in the most righteous and enlightened souls; and in the mysterious workshop where they tried to reproduce

[1] "Memoirs"—The Ecclesiastical History of the first Six Centuries.

in themselves the likeness of the Divine Image, more than one clumsy effort was abandoned, more than one rough sketch preluded the accomplishment of a final and lasting work.

Another characteristic distinguished Jerome from the Fathers with whom we have compared him. Ambrose confined himself to the journeys which the discharge of his duties, first as prefect and later as bishop, made imperative; neither did Augustine ever betray any tendency for travel. It is true that we can trace him from Tagastus to Madaura, from Madaura to Carthage, and from thence follow him to Rome, Milan, Cassiciacum and Ostia, to those shores which beheld the ecstasy of both mother and son, and which preserved the precious relics of the former until the fifteenth century. But these journeys were imposed upon him by necessity or by the responsibilities of his position; once returned to Africa, once installed in his episcopal town of Hippo, he never left it except when summoned to Carthage by the duties of his office, and he allowed his letters and works to be disseminated through the Roman Empire without him. He was completely indifferent to the spectacle of the outside world, and without neglecting either the modest flock to whom he brake the bread of the Word of God, or the countless souls who eagerly sought his teachings, he lived in the presence of the eternal truths; their horizon sufficed him and he desired no other! Jerome, on the other hand, unlike these two great men, was a born traveller. His eager and restless imagination, his adventurous temperament, led him from the borders of Dalmatia and Pannonia where he was born, and from Rome where he received his literary education, to Gaul, Asia and Egypt. The desire to learn rather than the desire to see, made an incessant pilgrimage of one portion of his life. We are told that he " undertook long and toilsome journeys throughout the Roman Empire, seeking to acquire in the society of men an experience which cannot be found in books, and halting at all the towns where there was anything to learn. We see him now at Trèves, which possessed one of the most flourishing schools in the West, now at Antioch or Constantinople. . He knew the three languages, Latin, Greek and Hebrew, and if his Greek was not as thorough as his Latin, at least he knew it as well as any other Roman of his period."[1] Jerome seems to have wished to justify his love of travel by citing the example of illustrious predecessors. " We read," he wrote Paulinus, " that people have been known to traverse provinces, cross seas, land among strange peoples, for the sake of seeing face to face those whom they knew only through their works. Thus did Pythagoras visit the wise men of Memphis, thus did Plato visit Egypt and Archytas of Tarentum, and at the cost of the rudest hardships travelled along the shores of that portion of the Italian coast which was then called Magna Græcia. He who in Athens was a powerful master became voluntarily a stranger and a disciple, preferring humbly to learn the thoughts of others, rather than rashly and imprudently impart his own."

[1] Henri Goelzer, "Lexicographical and Grammatical Study of the Latinity of St Jerome." Introduction, 1.

INTRODUCTORY

We must not forget that the knowledge which Jerome sought before all others was that of the Holy Writ and of tradition. To quote from Villemain: "This eager soul yearned to see at close range the birthplaces of religion and the summits on which its dawn first broke, and to question the teachers and anchorites of the Eastern Churches."[1] Jerome was the forerunner of all the pilgrims who have wished to begin or finish their studies of the Scriptures by a visit to the Holy Land. "One understands the Greek historians better after having seen Athens, and the third book of Virgil when one travels from Troas to Sicily, by Leucadia and the Acroceraunian mountains, and arrives at the mouth of the Tiber," wrote Jerome, "and in the same way one acquires a clearer insight into the Scriptures when one has seen Judæa with one's own eyes, evoked the memory of its decaying cities and learned the ancient and modern names which those famous places bear." (Ad Domnionem et Rogatianum in librum Paralipomenon Præfat.)

Such long and laborious researches were not fruitless. Returned for the last time to the desert and permanently established at Bethlehem close to the holy cave with which his memory was henceforth inseparably connected, he continued his work, which was occasionally interrupted by public and private calamity. He writes: "I was suddenly informed of the death of Pammachius and Marcella, of the siege of Rome and of the falling asleep in Jesus of so many

---

[1] Description of Christian eloquence in the fourth century.—St Jerome.

of my brothers and sisters in the faith. Appalled, I remained motionless, and for days and nights could think of nought but the deliverance of those dear to me. I shared, in imagination, the captivity of the Saints. I waited before opening my lips, to have more certain tidings of them. And after the light of the entire earth had been extinguished, after the power of the Roman Empire had been overthrown, or, to express it better, when in the fall of a single city the whole world had perished, I kept silence in my humiliation, I left unspoken what words of comfort I might have said, and my grief burst forth afresh. My heart kindled and burned within me whilst I meditated upon these things. I thought that I ought not to forget this sentence, 'An unseasonable discourse is like music during lamentation.'"[1]

The aged lion, however, rose again in his might; amongst the ruins which the invasion was heaping one upon another amid the tombs into which Nepotian, Fabiola, Pammachius, Marcella and Eustochium were lowered one by one, in spite of his grief at surviving these dear ones Jerome did not cease to write or dictate, and seemed to repeat, giving it a Christian interpretation, the motto of the Emperor Severus—"Laboremus." Death alone, to which he succumbed when over eighty years of age, relieved the intrepid veteran from the post of toil and battle which he had so long occupied. May those who wonder at, and are perhaps scandalised by the harshness of his language and the violence of his polemics, recall

[1] Commentary on Ezekiel. Lib. prim., 1, 2.

to their minds this lifetime entirely consecrated to study and to the defence of truth, which he loved with undivided devotion; then will astonishment tinged with distaste give way to a feeling of tender and grateful admiration.

THE LIFE OF SAINT JEROME

CHAPTER I

YOUTH

JEROME was born about the year 342 at Stridon, on the borders of Dalmatia and Pannonia, in the midst of a semi-barbaric population.[1] His parents, however, were wealthy Christians, and in a letter to Theophilus, the Patriarch of Alexandria, he testified to the pious care which from his earliest childhood had nourished him with the milk of the Catholic doctrine.[2] He was called Eusebius after his father, for Hieronymus or Heirome was merely a surname, or what in Latin is termed cognomen. His mother's name we do not know. Besides an aunt, Castorina, who seems to have shown him small affection,[3] Jerome had a sister, a cause of many anxieties, and one brother, Paulinian, whom he later took with him to Palestine from Rome.

The young Dalmatian began his studies at Stridon, and at the age of eighteen he went with Bonosus, a friend of his childhood, to continue them at Rome, where he attended the lessons of Donatus, the grammarian, and possibly those of Victorinus, whose

---

[1] De viris illustribus, cap. cxxxv.
[2] Epist. lxxii. ad Theophilum, 2.
[3] Epist. xiii. ad Castorinam Materteram

humble and courageous conversion has been immortalised in the Confessions of St Augustine.[1]

Reading, in which his eager soul found its outlet (he tells us himself that he studied Porphyry's Introduction, Alexander of Aphrodisias' Commentaries upon Aristotle, and Plato's Dialogues), completed his masters' teaching; and his passion for books, which he confesses were indispensable to him, enabled him to acquire, at the cost of the most arduous labour, that is by copying them with his own hand, an extensive library.[2] Thus was Jerome unconsciously preparing himself for the great works which were to fill his life.

He was as yet only a catechumen, for in those early centuries they frequently waited until the perilous ways of youth had been safely traversed before conferring baptism, and the Christian initiation was sometimes deferred from reasons of prudence. To know, however, that this prudence was liable to terrible mistakes one has only to recall the anguish of Gregory Nazianzen and of Satirus, St Ambrose's brother, who both, when overtaken by a tempest at sea, were terrified at the thought of dying unbaptised. It was especially the fear of the restraints imposed by the Christian life which deferred for years the baptism of many, and we are told by St Augustine that the deviations of the unbaptised were freely excused by a spirit of general tolerance.[3]

More fortunate in this respect than the son of

---

[1] Confession, lib. viii., cap. 11.
[2] Epist. xxii. ad Eustochium, 30.
[3] Confession, lib. i., c. xi.

Monica, Jerome, as he wrote to Theophilus of Alexandria, never fell into error. He used often to interrupt his studies in order to visit the basilicas of the Saints or to descend into the catacombs, and when an old man he thus described these pilgrimages in his "Commentaries upon Ezekiel." "In my youth, when I was studying literature in Rome, it was my custom to visit on Sundays, with some companions of my own age and tastes, the tombs of the martyrs and apostles. I often wandered into those subterranean galleries whose walls on either side preserve the relics of the dead, and where the darkness is so intense that one might almost believe that the words of the prophet had been fulfilled: 'Let them go down alive into hell.' A gleam of light shining through a narrow aperture, rather than a window, scarcely affected the awful obscurity, and the little band, shrouded in darkness and able only to proceed one step at a time, would recall this verse of Virgil's 'Everywhere horror and even the very silence appal me.'"[1]

In his youth Jerome witnessed the attempts made by Julian to restore paganism, and he saw also the utter failure in which they resulted. "While I was attending the schools of the grammarians," he wrote, "when every town was stained with the blood of idolatrous sacrifices, suddenly at the very height of the persecution Julian's death was announced to us. 'How,' exclaimed a pagan, and not unreasonably, 'do the Christians say that theirs is a patient and a merciful God? There is nothing more terrible,

[1] Comment. in Ezech., lib. xii., cxl.

nothing more swift than His wrath. He could not even for an instant defer His vengeance.' "[1]

The faith which had so early been instilled into Jerome and which was so precious to him, did not, however, shield him from the seductions of Rome, but unlike Augustine, who wrote the humble confession of his protracted sins, he only alludes to his in passing. "You know," he wrote Chromatius, "how slippery are those pathways of youth where I succumbed." In a letter to Heliodorus, whom he wished to take with him into the desert and whom he rebuked for his delay, he was more explicit: "Why linger in the world, thou who hast already chosen solitude? If I give thee this advice it is not as if my ship and my cargo were undamaged, not as if I were ignorant of the deep, but rather as one shipwrecked and just cast up upon the shore, in feeble tones I warn the navigators of their peril."[2]

There is another difference between Augustine and Jerome worthy of notice. It is evident that after the supreme struggles of which Augustine has given us a dramatic account, he experienced no further aggression of the vanquished foe. The luring voices which made one final effort to woo him to excess were silenced, and no doubt remained so for ever, for after his conversion Augustine seems to have inhabited serene heights inaccessible to any disturbing memories of the past; but Jerome, who was by nature more ardent and perhaps less gentle than the son of Monica, could not forget so quickly.

[1] Comment in Habacuc. Lib. ii. c. iii.
[2] Epist. xiv. ad Heliodorum, 6.

Beguiling visions followed him to the desert of Chalcis, and he succeeded in exorcising them only through ceaseless work and penances.

From Rome the young Dalmatian, with Bonosus, passed into Gaul and repaired to Trèves, where Valentinian I. then resided, and it was in Gaul that Jerome determined to renounce the world which had so wounded him, and devote himself to the service of Jesus Christ. He accordingly returned to Rome and was baptised there by Liberius. This Pope having died on the 24th of September 366, Jerome's baptism could not have taken place at a later date. Leaving Rome he started for Aquileia, where religious studies and monastic discipline flourished, and which was at that time an important town and the capital of its native province. Here he met many friends.

These friends monopolise a great part of Jerome's correspondence, but the place they held in his affections they did not all, alas! retain until the end. We will mention a few among them: Valerian, Bishop of Aquileia; Chromatius, Nicias, Jovinianus or Jovianus, who also became bishops; Chrysostom and Innocentius, called by Jerome the half of his soul, and Hylas, who, from being a freedman of the noble widow Melania, rose through the fellowship of a common vocation to the intimacy of men whose birth, learning, or fortune, had placed so far above him. Besides Bonosus, of whom we have already heard, there were two men at that time especially dear to Jerome—Heliodorus and Rufinus; the former famous through the earnest letter which Jerome wrote him trying to entice him into the desert, and because of the Episcopal virtues which he displayed, and the latter like Jerome himself, in turn a devoted friend and a bitter enemy, through quarrels, of which an account will be given.

Near Aquileia, at Concordia, a town now in ruins, the future translator and chronicler of Eusebius of Cæsarea met an aged man called Paul, who in his youth had known a secretary of St Cyprian's at Rome.[1] We quote here the charming letter in which Jerome, when sending him one of his works upon the holy writers, seems to have delighted in describing and praising the robust old age of this dweller in the remote past. "Behold, your hundredth year is passing, and ever faithful to the Saviour's precepts you find in present blessings a foretaste of the bliss to come. Your sight is clear, your steps firm, your hearing quick, your voice sonorous, and your body full of sap. Your rosy complexion contrasts with the whiteness of your hair, and your strength contradicts your years. Old age has not destroyed your memory, as with so many, nor a cooling blood blunted the keenness of your mind or extinguished its fire. No wrinkles furrow your brow or line your face. Your hand does not tremble: upon the waxen tablets it guides an unswerving stylus. God, who in your person illustrates the vigour and verdure of the future resurrection, has given us a lesson. If sin is the cause of others being already dead in the flesh although still alive, then your virtue has won you the privilege of still seeming young when of an age which is young no

[1] De viris illustribus. Cap. liii.

longer."[1] Jerome gathered much precious knowledge from Paul, whose wonderful and rare old age he so much admired. From him he learned that St Cyprian professed a keen admiration for Tertullian, whose works he daily read and whom he called his master. Thus through oral tradition Jerome began that study of church history to which he was later to contribute so largely.

His stay at Aquileia was only the first halt in a life of travel. From that time forth trials beset him. "He was already beginning," says Tillemont, "to make enemies whose persecutions were sufficiently violent to oblige him to move from place to place, and serious enough to reach the ears of the Pope Damasus."[2] One of his adversaries was the Bishop Lupicinus. Finally he determined to go to the East and, according to Baronius, before leaving the Western Hemisphere he paid a visit to his native town and there bade farewell to his own people for ever. He did not attempt to conceal the painful effort the breaking of these family ties cost him. "Whenever the impress of your familiar hands recalls your dear faces to me, then am I no longer where I am, or rather you are there with me."[3] The man who sent such a message, a message perhaps more touching than well expressed, to those from whom he was separated, the man who appreciated so keenly the bonds of friendship, was certainly not insensible to those

---

[1] Epist. x. ad Paulum Senem Concordiæ.
[2] Memoirs, etc., St Jerome. Article iv.
[3] Epist. vii. ad Chromatum Jovinum et Eusebium.

of blood. "Full well do I know," he wrote to Heliodorus, "what fetters hold thee back. My heart is not of stone nor my bowels of iron, I was not begotten by rocks nor suckled by the tigresses of Hyrcania; I also have gone through the anguish which thou dreadest."[1] Jerome probably had as travelling companions this same Heliodorus, and also Innocentius and Hylas, whom we again meet at his side in the East when, as Tillemont, who translated the works of the Saints, tells us: "He set out carrying with him the library he had collected in Rome, travelled over many provinces, passed through Thrace, Pontus and Bithynia, crossed the whole of Galatia and Cappadocia, suffered the intolerable heat of Cilicia . and finally in Syria found the peace which he sought as a safe harbour after shipwreck."

Before retiring into the desert, however, he spent a few days at Antioch with Evagrius, a priest of that city, whom Jerome had known in Italy, whither he had gone to lay the discords in his Church before the Western bishops, and who on his return became the guide and sponsor of Jerome and his companions in Antioch.

Jerome, inflamed with an ardour for study which never cooled, wished to hear the men most learned in the Scriptures, and especially Apollinaris, Bishop of Laodicea, who at that period had not yet fallen into his later notorious heresy. It was probably about this time that Jerome knew the hermit Malchus, but it was not until long after that he related his wonderful history, which Lafontaine has translated into graceful verse.

[1] Epist. xiv. ad Heliodorum, 3.

CHAPTER II

THE DESERT OF CHALCIS

JEROME, however, had left Aquileia, not for Antioch, but bound for the wilderness. He plunged into the heart of the desert of Chalcis, where, under burning skies and amid vast tracts of sand out of which sprang here and there a few scattered convents, he had gone to seek repentance, and where he found fresh sorrows awaiting him. Heliodorus returned to the West, and Jerome's friendship for Innocent and Hylas was ruthlessly severed by their death. But the memories of his libertine youth, which troubled the peace of his soul and threatened to sully a chastity so dearly bought, caused him a still keener grief than the loss of his friends, and he has left us a description of his anguish, of his almost desperate but finally victorious struggles, in pages of striking eloquence and immortal beauty. "How often," he wrote, "buried in this vast wilderness, scorched by the rays of the sun, have I imagined myself in the midst of the pleasures of Rome. I sat alone because my heart was filled with exceeding bitterness. My limbs were covered with unsightly sackcloth, and my blackened skin gave me the appearance of an Ethiopian. I wept and groaned daily, and if in spite of my struggles sleep overcame me, the bones in my emaciated body, which sank to the naked earth, barely clave together. I do not mention my nourishment or drink, for in this desert even the sick monks scarcely dare touch fresh water, and to eat cooked food would be considered an excess. And I, who, through the fear of hell, had condemned myself to this prison inhabited by scorpions and serpents, imagined myself transported into the midst of the dances of the young Roman maidens. My face was pallid with fasting, my body cold as ice, yet my soul burned with sensual emotion and in flesh already dead, only the fire of the passions was still capable of kindling. Debarred from all help I threw myself at the feet of Jesus, watered them with my tears, wiped them with my hair, and strove to subdue my rebellious flesh by weeks of abstinence. I do not blush to own to my misery, rather do I weep that I am no longer as I once was. I remember having often spent the entire day and night in crying aloud and in beating my breast, until, at the command of God, who rules the tempest, peace crept back into my soul. I even dreaded my cell as if it had been an accomplice to my thoughts. Angry with myself I penetrated alone further into the desert, and if I discovered any dark valley, any rugged mountain, any rock of difficult access, it was the spot I fixed upon to pray in, and to make into a prison for my wretched body. God is witness that sometimes, after having long fixed my eyes upon heaven, and after copious weeping. I believed myself transported among the choir of angels. Then in a trusting and joyful ecstasy I sang unto the Lord: 'We pursue Thee by the scent of Thy perfumes.'"[1]

In order to subdue his flesh and curb his imagination, Jerome had recourse to other means besides corporal punishment. "When I was young," he wrote, "although buried in the desert, I could not conquer my burning passions and ardent nature, and in spite of my body being exhausted by perpetual fasts my brain was on fire with evil thoughts. Finally, as a last resource, I put myself under the tutelage of a certain monk, a Jew who had become a Christian, and, forsaking the ingenious precepts of Quintilian, the floods of eloquence poured forth by Cicero, the grave utterances of Fronto, and the tender words of Pliny, I began to learn the Hebrew alphabet, and to study this language of hissing and harsh-sounding words. I who have suffered so much, and with me those who at that time shared my life, can alone testify to the efforts I wasted, the difficulties I went through, and how often I despairingly interrupted my studies, which a dogged determination to learn made me afterwards resume; and I give thanks unto God that from such a bitter sowing I am now able to gather such sweet fruit."[2]

It was probably at this period, that is in 374, that the mysterious dream of which Jerome has left us a dramatic account came to him. Imbued with the works of classic antiquity, he cherished a love

Epist. xxii. ad Eustochium, 7.
Epist. cxxv. ad Rusticum monachum, 12.

for them. "Miserable wretch," he wrote, "I fasted before reading Cicero, after nights spent in vigil, after tears wrung from me by the memory of my sins, I would take up Plautus, and when, on coming to my senses, I read the Prophets, their speech seemed to me uncouth and unfinished. Blind, I blamed the light instead of condemning my own eyes." A vision cured him, for a while at least, of this passion. "Towards the middle of Lent (probably the Lent of 375), while Satan was thus mocking me, I was seized with a fever which, finding my body exhausted by want of rest, consumed it to such an extent that my bones barely clave together. My body was becoming cold, a faint remnant of warmth however still enabled my heart to beat. They were preparing my funeral obsequies, when suddenly my soul was caught up from me and carried before the Tribunal of the Supreme Judge. The light was so dazzling, those who surrounded Him shed such a blaze of splendour, that, falling back upon the ground, I dared not gaze aloft. They asked me who I was and I answered a Christian. 'Thou liest,' said the Judge, 'thou art a Ciceronian and not a Christian, for where thy treasure is, there is thy heart also.' I was silent; and whilst the blows rained down upon me, for the Judge had commanded that I should be scourged, suffering even more from the torment of my bitter remorse, I repeated to myself this verse of the Psalms: 'Who will render thee glory in hell?' Then I cried out weeping: 'Have pity on me, Lord, have pity.' This cry rang out in the midst of the blows, and at last those who were present, throwing themselves at the feet of the Judge, entreated Him to have mercy upon my youth, to grant me time to work out my repentance, and to punish me severely if I should again peruse a pagan book. I, who, to escape from the terrible straits in which I found myself would have promised far more, swore to Him and said, calling His name to witness: 'Lord, if hereafter I harbour or read any secular books, may I be treated as if I had renounced Thee.' After this oath I was released and I returned to earth. Those present were astonished to see me reopen my eyes, which were bathed in such a flood of tears that my grief convinced the most sceptical. That it was not one of those vain dreams by which we are deceived, I attest the Tribunal before which I lay prostrate and the sentence which so appalled me. Please God that I may never again be submitted to such an ordeal. When I awoke my shoulders were bruised and I could still feel the blows. From that moment I studied religious books with far more ardour than I had ever read profane ones."[1]

Did Jerome abide by this oath throughout his life? Although making allowances for the Saint's vigorous memory, to which reminiscences of Terence, Lucretius, Cicero, Virgil and Seneca were continually recurring (Augustine, at Hippo, preserved the memory of his classical education in the same tenacious manner), we have reason to believe that Jerome more than once opened the works of these pagan authors whom he had renounced. To Rufinus, whose insidious hatred accused him of the crime of

[1] Epist. xxii. ad Eustochium, 30.

perjury, he replied that the keeping of a promise made in a dream could not be exacted of him. However, even if Jerome did not deem himself irrevocably bound by his pledge, he applied himself more and more to the study of the Bible, and his classical reading and recollections were exclusively devoted to defending and embellishing the truth. This is what he pointed out in a celebrated letter to Magnus, the orator, in which, with skilful and weighty arguments he cited the example of all his predecessors, reminding him that according to Deuteronomy the Israelite must needs cut the nails and hair of his slave before marrying her. " Is it astonishing that profane literature should have seduced me by the grace of its language and by the beauty of its form, or that I should wish to convert a slave and a captive into a daughter of Israel? If I come across anything dead, any passage breathing idolatry, sensuality, error, or evil passions, I suppress it, and from my alliance with a stainless spouse are born servants of the true God; thus do I increase the family of Christ."[1]

The questions of discipline and dogma which were agitating the Church of Antioch, disturbed Jerome afresh in his retreat. Four bishops were contending for the Patriarchal See of the East. In 361, after the death of Eustathius, the intrepid champion of the Nicean faith, the Arians and many Catholics had agreed to elect Meletius of Sebaste, whose orthodoxy, already attested at the time of Constantine's persecution, asserted itself at Antioch

[1] Epist. lxx. ad Magnum, oratorem urbis Romæ, 2.

from the very first, with the result of alienating the Arians, who chose Euzoïus as their leader. Those Catholics, however, who were most devoted to Eustathius' glorious memory, refused to give their support to a bishop who had counted Arians among his electors. Towards the end of 379 Lucifer of Cagliari, on his return from the exile to which he had been banished by the son of Constantine, appointed the priest Paulinus, who was recognised by Alexandria and the West, as Bishop to the *Eustathians*. At the beginning of 376, to support his heresy in introducing the Bishop of Laodicea into Antioch, Apollinaris had the audacity to assign the government of this great Church to his disciple Vitalis, whom he had consecrated. Quite outside of all this, the inhabitants of Antioch and of the monasteries at Chalcis were discussing whether they should recognise in God three hypostases or three persons. In the theological language of to-day the two terms are synonymous, but in the fourth century they were not considered so by all. At Antioch the Meletians used the word hypostasis in preference to the word person, a form which Sabellius had not refuted; the partisans of Paulinus, on the other hand, conforming themselves to the Latin custom which understood hypostasis and substance to be synonymous, considered it an Arian impiety to say that in God there were three hypostases. Urged by the monks amongst whom he lived to pronounce upon the legitimate vicar and the orthodox expression, Jerome addressed himself in two famous letters to the Pope Damasus. Certainly these letters are sufficient proof that he disliked the word hypostasis, which seemed to him equivocal or erroneous. Meletius too, the champion of this word, was especially displeasing to him, and his sympathies were entirely drawn towards Paulinus, the patriarch favoured by Latin Christianity. Upon these points he asked the judgment of the Roman Pontiff, which he valued above everything, and to which he was willing to submit. "I thought," he wrote Damasus, that I ought to consult the Apostolic See and the Roman Faith which St Paul the Apostle extolled. I crave spiritual nourishment from the Church where I received the baptismal robe. . . You are the light of the world, the salt of the earth, in your possession are the vessels of silver and gold, elsewhere are the vessels of clay and of wood destined for the iron rod which shall shatter them, and for the eternal fires which shall consume them."

In terms which succeeding centuries have freely quoted, Jerome proclaimed the Roman pre-eminence and the obligation imposed upon all to conform to it. "I know that on that stone the Church was built; he who eats of the Paschal Lamb outside of its walls is an impious man. He who has not sought refuge in the Ark of Noah will be overtaken by the deluge." He then asked Damasus to inform him which vicar he was to follow and which term he was to employ. "I do not know Vitalis, I repudiate Meletius, I ignore Paulinus. Whoever reaps not with thee, scatters; whoever belongs not to Christ belongs to Antichrist." It is evident that Jerome could not accept the term hypostasis with enthusiasm; he declares as much in bitter, almost haughty tones; nevertheless he was willing to accept it should Damasus pronounce its usage to be legitimate. "I pray you decide this matter for me, and I will not shrink from saying that there are three hypostases in God. . I implore your Holiness by the crucified Lord, by the consubstantial Trinity, to write and authorise me either to suppress or use this word."[1]

Jerome left Chalcis, probably driven from the desert by some foolish persecution, and joined Evagrius in Antioch, where Paulinus compelled him to enter the priesthood; but so strong was his love of solitude, so jealous was he of his liberty, that he stipulated that his ordination should not bind him to any one particular church. By a peculiarity which the Jansenists willingly proposed as a model, Jerome never ascended to the altar. In virtue of this liberty which was justly dear to him, he contended, in a dialogue written at Antioch, against the heterodox rigorism of Lucifer of Cagliari, the bishop who had consecrated his friend Paulinus.

Towards 380 we meet the indefatigable traveller at Constantinople, where St Gregory of Nazianzus, placed against his will upon the episcopal throne of that town, was re-establishing the true faith in the hearts of a people who for forty years had been given over to Arianism, and with poetic and touching eloquence was distributing the treasures of his irreproachable doctrine among them. It was to the tuition of such a master that Jerome submitted him-

[1] Epist. xv. ad Damasum papam.

self, and in after years he took pleasure in evoking his reminiscences of him, and in repeating his lessons.

He also knew at that time another Doctor of the Church, St Gregory of Nyssa, St Basil's brother, who read him his refutation of Eunomius and of Anomoeanism, that audacious and radical form of the Arian error. Eunomius and his adherents represented in fact the left wing of Arianism, and as has already been said they extricated the latent rationalism from this heresy. The name of Anomoean (ἀνόμοιος) which they had adopted, was a protest not only against the ὁμοούσιος of the Catholics, who proclaim the Son to be of the same substance as the Father, but also against the ὁμοιούσιος of the semi-Arians, who declared the substance of the Son to be like that of the Father. This name signified that, according to their idea, the Son was neither equal to nor like the Father. Thus was God leading the future interpreter of the Scriptures to the purest and most abundant fountain heads of Catholic teaching and placing him amongst men to whom heresy was familiar and who excelled in confuting it. He was about to bring him into the very heart of truth, for Gregory of Nazianzus, disheartened by the weakness and ingratitude of man, and anxious to return to his solitude of Arianze, had, at the Council of 381, abdicated his Episcopacy; there being now nothing further to detain Jerome at Constantinople he started for Rome, where the Council which Pope Damasus had convoked seemed to call back into the Church of his baptism this Dalmatian, ripened by age, penance and study, and especially fitted to give to the supreme authority information regarding the disciplinarian and dogmatic controversies then agitating the patriarchate of Antioch. On his way, Jerome, according to Baronius, must have passed through Greece, and it is to this period, that is towards the year 382, that we must ascribe a journey of which we have but few details. " It is strange," it has been said, " that our Saint should not have told us more of a country in which it is impossible to walk a step without awakening a host of memories. Did he fear that his journey was in some way an occult sacrifice to his admiration for the antique, a secret homage to the pagan spirit whose influence he seemed so much to dread, or did he recall the words of his revered master?"[1] This master, Gregory Nazianzen, so Greek in his genius and in his language, certainly seems to have harboured against Athens, where he had feasted upon the masterpieces of antiquity, the same feelings of anxious distrust which many centuries later Manning experienced about the Oxford of his youth. Let us say, in short, without more circumlocutions, that Jerome, wedded though he was to Greek literature, was not in his turn of mind one of those baptized sons of Hellas who, under the neophite's robe or even under that of the priest or pontiff, remain ever faithful to this revealer of so much beauty, and are always ready to turn towards it gratefully and almost tenderly. Jerome would never have exclaimed, as did Fenelon at the beginning of his career in a letter to Bossuet, full of lively and charming spontaneity interspersed with reminiscences

[1] "Journeys of St Jerome," by Eugene Bernard. Chap. iv. 3.

and aspirations of the most varied description: "I am about to start, I very nearly fly... The whole of Greece lies open before me, the Sultan draws back in alarm, already the Peloponnesus breathes in liberty and the Corinthian Church bursts into new life; the voice of the Apostle shall once more be heard within it. I feel myself transported into those lovely spots, those precious ruins, and collecting there, not only the most curious monuments but the very spirit of antiquity itself. I seek the Areopagus where Paul proclaimed the unknown God to the wise men of the world, but after the sacred comes the profane and I do not disdain to pause at Piraeus, where Socrates planned his republic. I ascend the double summit of Parnassus, I pluck the laurels of Delphi and I taste the delights of Tempe."

It is not in this manner that Jerome speaks of Corinth, although he praises its literary taste, cultivated by its proximity to Attica, or even of Athens. If he mentions this town which, according to a famous saying, is the very Greece of Greece, it was merely to say that he had seen, near the statue of Minerva, a brazen sphere so heavy that he could scarcely move it. "I asked," he adds, "what was the use of this sphere, and they answered that it served to test the strength of the athletes, and that no one could enter the arena without having lifted this weight, thereby showing which antagonist he was fitted to encounter."[1] In another commentary he alludes to the Athenian altar whose mysterious superscription suggested such a persuasive exordium

[1] Commentar. in Zachariam. Lib. iii., cap. xii. v. 11.

to St Paul. "The inscription," said Jerome, "did not run 'To the unknown God,' but 'To the Gods of Asia and Africa, to the unknown and foreign Gods!' As Paul only needed to mention one unknown God he employed the singular when he informed the Athenians that this God designated in the inscription on their altar, was his own; and when he enabled them henceforward to know and worthily honour the God whom they could not ignore and whom they unconsciously worshipped."[1] This statement, if correct (for Pausanius the geographer quotes a similar inscription to that mentioned by St Paul), is an example of how ingeniously, if somewhat unscrupulously, this Apostle, who excited such a keen interest in Jerome, as indeed he still does in us, profited by every opportunity that lay within his reach.

[1] Commentar. in Epist. ad Titum. I. v. 10, 11.

CHAPTER III

ROME

JEROME arrived in Rome accompanied by two Eastern bishops, Paulinus to whom he adhered, and Epiphanius of Salamis. Important work, illustrious friendships, struggles, and also bitter trials, awaited him in the capital of the Christian world. At the council which Damasus convoked Jerome gave evidence of his erudition and of the soundness of his doctrine in defending, with the authority of St Athanasius, a name ascribed to Christ (*homo dominicus*), the orthodoxy of which was contested by the Apollinarists. The Pope, impressed by the talent he was well fitted to appreciate, made Jerome his Secretary, empowered him to reply in his name to the inquiries of the Synods, and often referred to the wisdom of the learned exegete on his own account. Further, Damasus forcibly influenced the whole life of his collaborator. He had seen his tendency to omnivorous reading, an occupation insufficiently stimulating to the mind, which suggested to Father Gratry this pithy sally: "Oh! reading! idleness in disguise!"; and he roused him from this beguiling torpor by urging him to useful work. At his request Jerome translated two of Origen's Homilies on the Song of Solomon, and began to translate the treatise upon the Holy Ghost, by Didymus, the blind sage of Alexandria. Was it St Ambrose's work on the same subject which Jerome criticised in such severe terms in his Preface? ("Nihil ibi dialecticum nihil virile atque districtum . . . sed totum flaccidum, molle. . ."). Rufinus in his Invectives pretended that it was, but the Benedictines who edited the Bishop of Milan's work disputed this assertion, which Tillemont, however, seems inclined to believe.[1] From the pen of such a censor as Jerome the harshest criticisms are by no means surprising, and this was especially a criticism of a literary order.

Damasus exacted a task of still greater importance from Jerome. The Gospel had at an early date been translated into Latin for the benefit of Western Christianity, but the primitive version, the ancient Itala, had suffered in the manuscripts in circulation corrections, and also innumerable alterations and additions. Moreover, through the need of a concordance, in order to make the copy already owned as complete as possible, the various narratives of the Evangelists were frequently united in a single text. Alarmed at the danger introduced by these divergencies, Damasus entreated Jerome to revise the New Testament according to the original Greek. Jerome, who was by nature intolerant of contradiction, had no illusions as to the criticism to which this task would expose him. He was about to disturb old ways of thought, and possibly startle timid consciences; nevertheless, strong in the support

[1] Memoirs, etc., St Ambrose. Note xi.

afforded him by the Pope, he began and successfully terminated the work demanded of him, suppressed the interpolations, re-established the inverted sequence of the sacred text, and presented this meritorious achievement to Damasus, having added to it the ten canons or tables of concordance translated from Greek into Latin, in which Eusebius of Cæsarea, and later Ammonius of Alexandria, had shown what was special to each Evangelist and what was common to all four.

Jerome undertook another revision, that of the Psalter. The translation current in the Latin Church had been made from the Greek text of the Septuagint, but owing to the numerous alterations which had crept into the manuscript copies, it was incorrect in many places. From the Hieronymian revision sprang the Psalterium Romanum, which was in use in Rome up to the reign of St Pius V., and to which the Venite Exultemus in the Invitatory and the passages of the Psalms cited in the missal still belong. "This first work was in its turn soon altered by the copyists, and at the urgent desire of St Paula, Jerome decided to make a second revision, which this time he based upon Origen's Hexapla. This was the Psalterium Gallicanum (anno 389), so called because it was first adopted in Gaul.

The Gallican Psalter is the one inserted in our Vulgate and used in our Breviary."[1] Somewhat later, about 392, he translated the Psalms from the Hebrew.

These works, and the austerity of Jerome's life

[1] Abbé Lesêtre.—Introduction to the Book of Psalms.

while accomplishing them, drew much attention upon the secretary of Pope Damasus, and won him many illustrious and priceless friendships.

In a palace on the Aventine, one of the Seven Hills of Rome, some noble-hearted women of earnest faith, striving to attain the evangelical ideal, gathered together and confronted the paganism which was still general, and the immorality of an all too large number of Christians, with the humble and courageous exhibition of their virtue. The mistress of this noble dwelling was Marcella, who had consecrated her premature and irrevocable widowhood to God, to the poor, and to the study of holy works. With her were also her mother, Albina, Asella, whose meekness was extolled by Palladius the historian of St John Chrysostom; Furia, the heiress of the Camilli, Fabiola, who, although less strong in righteousness than her pious comrades, eventually atoned for the sins of her youth by penance and charity, Lea, the widow, and Principia.

We must especially mention three women who were more cherished by Jerome than all the others, and whose names are closely linked with his in history, namely Paula and two of her daughters, Blesilla and Eustochium.

It is unnecessary here to give an account of Paula's early history. By her mother she was authentically connected with the Scipios and the Gracchi, and her father, Rogatus, a wealthy proprietor of Nicopolis, claimed descent from Agamemnon, the king of kings. At the age of thirty-five, after the death of her husband, Julius Toxotius a reputed descendant of Æneas, for in the genealogy of patrician Rome legend blends easily with history, Paula was inspired by Marcella's example to adopt the ascetic life, in which she soon equalled her heroic friend. Her eldest daughter, Blesilla, left a widow after seven months of marriage, re-entered the narrow path from which the world had momentarily tempted her, and died in the flower of her youth, lamented in pathetic accents by Jerome. "Who," he exclaimed, "will bestow upon mine eyes a spring of tears that I may weep, not like Jeremiah for the wounded of my people, nor even like Jesus over the sorrows of Jerusalem, but over saintliness and mercy, innocence and chastity, all the virtues laid low in the death of one being. Not that we need weep for her who is departed, but rather for ourselves who have ceased to see her. Who could recall with dry eyes this youthful woman of twenty, whose ardent faith raised aloft the standard of the Crucified? Who could remember unmoved her persistency in prayer, the beauty of her language, the accuracy of her memory and the acuteness of her mind? Had you heard her speak Greek you would have supposed that she knew no Latin; when she conversed in Latin, no unfamiliarity with that tongue could be detected in her speech. And, marvellous gift which the whole of Greece admired in Origen, in a few days she had overcome the difficulties of the Hebrew tongue to such an extent that she vied with her mother in the study and in the singing of the Psalms. The poverty of her raiment was not a cloak to pride, as in the case of so many; genuinely humble, she made no effort to distinguish herself from among the women who surrounded her, except by a greater forgetfulness of self. Weakened by suffering, Blesilla dragged herself about, pale and trembling, barely able to raise her head, yet always holding in her hand either the Prophets or the Gospel. . Consumed by fever and at her last gasp, she addressed her supreme request to those nearest to her: " Ask the Lord Jesus to forgive me for not having fulfilled my intention" (Blesilla had contemplated entering the monastic life). Rest in peace, oh Blesilla! thy garments are white and will always remain so; their spotless purity is the splendour of eternal virginity." " We may be assured," pursues St Jerome, "that Blesilla was converted"; (in Christian parlance, in that of a St Philip Neri, who was continually having masses celebrated for his conversion, 'Conversion' does not necessarily signify the transition from sin to grace;) " for as long as this life lasts no conversion ever comes too late. It was to the crucified thief that these words were originally said, 'To-day shalt thou be with me in Paradise.' When Blesilla had laid down the burden of her perishable flesh, when her soul, returning from a long exile, had soared to its Creator and had entered upon the eternal inheritance, magnificent obsequies were celebrated in her honour and a long procession of patricians followed her coffin, over which was spread a golden veil, to the sepulchre. But I thought that I heard from the height of heaven Blesilla crying to me: ' I do not recognise such raiment; these funeral trappings are not for me; this pomp does not concern me.'"

"But what am I doing?" continued Jerome, "I forbid a mother to weep yet I weep myself; I acknowledge my sorrow, the page upon which I write is wet with my tears. But did not Jesus weep for Lazarus because he loved him? . . I call to witness, Oh Paula, the Jesus whom Blesilla followed, the angels whose companion she has now become, that I suffer the same grief which is rending you. She was my child of the spirit; I nourished her with the milk of my charity; and there were moments when I cried, 'Perish the day when I was born.'"[1] Then the Saint soars to lofty meditations upon the unfathomable mysteries of the divine government.

Eustochium, another of Paula's daughters, was reserved for a longer career than Blesilla, the tenderly-mourned. She followed her mother to the East, where she succeeded her in the direction of the convents in Palestine, and, always calm, always invincible to temptation, she retained Jerome as consoler and guide until the end.

The love of the Scriptures glowed in the hearts of these Christian women who, in order to acquire a deeper knowledge of the holy books, resolutely began the study of Greek and Hebrew. In these researches, where the knowledge of truth and not the elusive joys of vainglory were sought, they were directed by Jerome; and Marcella, whose guest he had become, outstripped all her companions in

[1] Epist. xxxix. ad Paulam, 1, 2.

this arduous pursuit. Later on, the recluse of Bethlehem, in his "Commentary on the Epistle to the Ephesians," wrote of her: "Whenever I picture to myself her ardour for study, her vivacity of mind and her application, I blame my idleness, I who, retreated in this wilderness, with the manger whither the shepherds came in haste to adore the wailing Christ-child constantly before mine eyes, am unable to accomplish what a noble woman accomplishes in the hour she snatches from the cares of a large circle and the government of her household."

Jerome was reproached for teaching only women. He answered what too often, alas, the priest of the present day would have the right to reply: "If men questioned me more about the Scriptures I would speak less to women." He added: "I rejoice, I am filled with enthusiasm, when in Babylon I meet Daniel, Ananias, Azarias, and Misaël."[1] He found Daniel, Ananias, Azarias, and Misaël in a few chosen friends who frequented the Aventine and attended the religious school. They were Pammachius, Marcella's cousin, who was to marry Paulina, Paula's second daughter; Oceanus, a learned man who later visited Jerome at Bethlehem; Marcellinus, who in Africa, in the time of Augustine, was the most conscientious of magistrates; and Domnion, a priest advanced in years, the praises of whose charity were sung by all.

In spite of the austere sweetness of these friendships, in spite of the substantial support which the protection of Damasus secured for him, Jerome did

[1] Epist. lxv. ad Principiam virginem, 2.

not taste peace in Rome. Was peace, however, what he sought? Jerome surely did not shrink from contention. He had defended the incomparable benefits of perfect chastity against Helvidius, a contemner of the dogma of the perpetual virginity of Mary, and, without denying the legitimacy of marriage, he pointed out its drawbacks, I was about to say its evils. He encouraged young girls, for whom honourable or brilliant marriages were in contemplation, in their desire to lead a monastic life, and at the sight of the Roman virgins who, through his advice, thus renounced their families, there were many who would readily have accused him of murder, more especially after the death of Blesilla, whom he was reported to have killed by dint of the fasts he imposed upon her. That was not the only grudge harboured against him. He denounced with eloquent indignation and inexhaustible fervour the licentiousness, avarice, intemperance and hypocrisy which had crept in among the priests and the monks at Rome, and it may easily be imagined that those stung by his powerful satire, and those who recognised themselves or were recognised by others in his portraits, became incensed, and that anger and resentment broke out against him on every side. Calumny soon came to the aid of spite, and at the expense of all justice as well as truth, the relations between Paula and her spiritual director were incriminated. The death of Damasus, which took place on the 11th of December 384, deprived Jerome of his protector, excluded him from the Apostolic Chancery, and completed his severance from Rome. His thoughts turned once more to the desert, but this time it was the biblical desert in which he wished permanently to establish himself, and he left Rome for ever, taking with him his brother Paulinian, the priest Vincent, and a few monks. From Ostia, on the point of embarking, he wrote a letter to Asella, in which his affectionate and saddened soul reveals itself. " If I believed myself capable of thanking thee worthily," he wrote, " I should be incensed. But God can reward thy saintly soul for me for the good thou hast done me. As to me, I am unworthy of it, and I never had any right to hope or even to wish that thou wouldest grant me in Jesus Christ so great an affection. And even if certain persons believe me to be a vile wretch overwhelmed by the weight of my sins —in comparison to my sins that is but little—yet thou art right in letting thy heart distinguish for thee between the righteous and the unrighteous. . ." Jerome then proceeded to exonerate himself from the calumnies which had assailed him and invoked the memory and testimony of Asella and of all those who lived on the Aventine. " Many a time have I been surrounded by a flock of virgins, and to the best of my ability expounded the divine books to several of them. Study creates assiduity, assiduity familiarity, and familiarity a mutual understanding. Call upon those virgins to answer if they have ever had any thought from me other than those one should receive from a Christian. Have I ever taken money from any of them? Have I not always repulsed every gift large or small? Has my neighbour's lucre ever soiled my hand? Have I ever uttered a dubious word or cast too bold a glance?" In conclusion Jerome sends a supreme farewell to the women he was leaving in Rome. "Greet Paula and Eustochium, who are my sisters in Christ whether the world so wills it or not, greet Albina my mother, Marcella my sister, and also Marcellina and Felicitas, and say to them that we shall all appear together at the judgment seat of Christ. Then shall be revealed the inner conscience and the life of each. Keep me in thy thoughts, oh model of virginal purity, and may thy prayers subdue the angry waves upon my way!"[1]

Even before the severe trials which had come to her, Paula had contemplated leaving Rome. She had been inspired by the descriptions of Paulinus of Antioch, and of Epiphanius of Salamis, whom she had received into her home at the time of the Roman Council of 382, to visit the cradle of religion in the East, where she yearned to behold the places consecrated by the mortal life of our Lord. From early days, but especially after the reign of Constantine, many Christians had visited Palestine. Helena's pilgrimage lives in every memory. Paula also wished to make hers, but in her heart she intended it to be a pilgrimage from which she should never return. Jerome led the way. "He journeyed to Rhegium," says Tillemont, "and after crossing the famous straits of Messina between Scylla and Charybdis he encircled the Cape of

[1] Epist. xlv. ad Asellam.

Malea, crossed the sea of Cyclades and landed at Cyprus, where he was received by St Epiphanius, the Bishop of Salamis. From thence he proceeded to Antioch, where he remained with Paulinus until the middle of the winter."[1]

Accompanied by Eustochium and a band of Roman maidens who had also dedicated their lives to virginity, Paula tore herself from the endearments and tears of her other children Toxotius and Rufina, who from the shore strove in vain to detain her, and after a brief sojourn in the island of Pontus, whither Flavia Domitilla, a relation of the Emperor Domitian, had been exiled on account of her faith, and a rest of ten days in Cyprus, where St Epiphanius returned to his guest the hospitality he had received from her in Rome, the noble woman reached Antioch. Here Paulinus would fain have persuaded her to stop a while, but she was impatient to start for Jerusalem, and, in spite of the winter, she set forth across rough country travelling upon an ass, she who, as Jerome said, had formerly never walked except supported upon the arms of her servants. "It is probable," says Tillemont, "that Jerome made this journey in the company of St Paula, with whom he certainly was when she arrived in Bethlehem."[2]

We will not go into their itinerary, nor describe Paula's raptures when she found herself standing upon Calvary or at the tomb of our Lord. After Jerusalem the pilgrims visited Bethlehem. "Miserable sinner," cried Paula, "I have been deemed

[1] Memoirs, etc., St Jerome. Chap. xlii.   [2] *Ibid.* Art. xiii.

worthy of kissing the manger wherein my infant Saviour lay, and of praying in the cave where the Virgin Mother gave birth to our Lord. This is my resting-place, for this is the country of my God. I shall inhabit the dwelling which my Lord selected for Himself."[1] As a matter of fact it was in Bethlehem that Paula was to live and die; it was there also that Jerome was about to settle.

Our travellers however, before permanently establishing themselves in the cave of the Nativity proceeded to Egypt, and the land of the Pharaohs, where the Holy family had found shelter, and where so many ascetics seemed by the heroic excesses of their penances to defy nature and place themselves on the level of angels, was to Paula and her guide a second Holy Land. Jerome had still another reason for visiting Egypt; he was anxious to consult the blind Didymus, at that time the most illustrious representative of the school of Alexandria. "My head," he wrote, "was beginning to be covered with gray hairs, which better become a master than a pupil, yet I became a disciple of Didymus, and I have every cause to be thankful to him. . ."[2] Jerome's intense love of travel, or rather Providence which directs secondary causes without forcing them, led him to Alexandria, after having taken him to Antioch, Constantinople and Rome, so that no cradle of tradition or of Catholic science should be unknown to him.

[1] Epist. cviii. ad Eustochium, 10.
[2] Epist. lxxxiv. Pammachio et Oceano.

CHAPTER IV

BETHLEHEM—YEARS OF PEACE

THE traveller returned to Palestine and established himself at Bethlehem, where, out of the wreck of his inheritance, consisting of farms partially destroyed by the barbarians, which Paulinian was commissioned to sell, and with the aid of Paula's bounty, he erected a monastery which he fortified with a tower of refuge. He selected for his cell a cave close to the one where our Lord was born. Paula, meanwhile, after having built some temporary cells, was engaged in constructing convents, and her indefatigable charity endowed as a hospice for pilgrims the hamlet where, as Jerome observed, Mary and Joseph had been without shelter.

In Palestine Jerome was once more thrown with Rufinus, a friend of his youth, who had left Rome in 371 and after six years spent in Egypt had settled at Jerusalem not far from the widow Melania, celebrated for her austere sacrifices and her continual journeys. The intimacy which absence had interrupted without destroying, was renewed between the two friends. Jerome used even to have the manuscripts of secular literature needed for his disciples copied by the monks belonging to the convent of the Olive Trees, which Rufinus directed.

The early days of Jerome's sojourn in Bethlehem were most serene; everything charmed and satisfied him, and a tremour of joyous admiration, a breath of spring, one might almost say, seems to vibrate through the pages which he wrote or inspired during that period. "The most illustrious Gauls congregate here, and no sooner has the Briton, so remote from our world, made any progress in piety, than he abandons his early setting sun to seek a land which he knows only by reputation, and through the Scriptures. And what of the Armenians, the Persians, the nations of India and Ethiopia; of Egypt herself, so rich in monks, of Pontus, Cappadocia, Cœlesyria and Mesopotamia? All these Eastern countries send us hordes of monks .
they throng here and set us the example of every virtue. The languages differ but the religion is the same, and one can count as many different choirs singing the psalms as there are nations. Yet in all this—and this is the triumph of Christianity—there is no vainglory, none prides himself upon his chastity; if they quarrel it is as to who shall be the humblest, for the last is here counted first. .
They do not judge one another, for fear of being judged by the Saviour, and slander, so prevalent in many districts where they malign each other outrageously, is here completely unknown. Here is no luxury, no sensuality. . ." Either Jerome or Paula closes this description with a few lines of idyllic grace. "In this land of Christ's all is simplicity, and except when the Psalms are being sung all is silence. Wherever you may go you hear the

labourer, with his hand upon the plough, murmuring Alleluia. The reaper, with the sweat pouring from his brow, finds relaxation in singing the Psalms, and the vintager recites some passage from David while pruning his vines. They are, so to speak, the love songs of the country; the shepherds' lilt, the labourers' accompaniment." [1]

These peaceful years were also years of toil for Jerome. The direction of the convents which had sprung up about the cave of Bethlehem, the active correspondence he maintained with his friends in the outer world, even the grammatical instruction he gave to the young men, which brought back to him those secular works of antiquity he had vainly striven to hate or to forget, would have been sufficient in themselves to fill his life. They were, however, but a minor portion of his work. He had undertaken the study of the Scriptures at the advice of Damasus, but the providential attraction which also drew him to them, was continually growing stronger and surer. Everything seemed to lead him to the Bible. The Abbé Eugène Bernard, in the eighth chapter of his "Journeys of St Jerome," says that "his letters were commentaries on the Bible.

If he interested himself in history or geography, it was in order to gain a more exact knowledge of the land where the events of the Old and the New Testament had taken place." To better understand the sacred books he resumed his study of Hebrew, and added to it the study of Chaldaic, and this language, in which are written the book of Tobias and part of the

[1] Epist. xlvi.—Paulæ et Eustochii ad Marcellam, 9, 10, 11.

book of Daniel, cost him infinite pains. " I lately," he wrote, " came to a standstill in the book of Daniel, and I experienced such a feeling of vexation that, suddenly seized with despair, I was tempted to look upon everything I had hitherto done as useless. A Jew, however, encouraged me. He repeated so often in his own tongue the " Labor omnia vincit improbus " that I, who was considered a master in Hebrew, became a scholar in order to learn Chaldaic. It is true that I read and understand this language better than I speak it."[1]

Paula and Eustochium, who were already initiated into the intricacies of the Hebrew tongue, assisted Jerome in his work. They read the Bible with him, and their pious and insatiable thirst for knowledge provoked explanations which the Saint, by his own confession, took from the Masters of the Faith, with whom no one was more familiar than he. At their desire he commentated the Epistles to Philemon, to the Galatians, to the Ephesians, and to Titus, and he completed for these two survivors of Blesilla the explanation of Ecclesiasticus for which she had formerly (386-387) asked him. " He translated the text from the Hebrew, keeping as much as possible to the Septuagint. Sixtus of Sienna considered it an admirable work, owing to the brevity and lucidity with which he expounded the spiritual and literal meaning."[2]

Jerome was also engaged in many other literary labours, such as the translation of thirty-nine of

[1] Præfatio Hieronymi in Danielem prophetam.
[2] Tillemont.—Memoirs, etc., St Jerome. Art. xlviii.

Origen's Homilies upon St Luke, and the long interrupted translation of the treatise of Didymus upon the Holy Ghost, a treatise on Hebrew names and places, another on Hebraical questions, an essay on etymology and biblical geography, a biography of the illustrious men in the Church, and finally protests against the monk Jovinianus, who contested the excellence of virginity and added other errors to this profoundly unchristian one, notably that of the parity of sins and the equality of merits.

In the midst of these many works the study and the interpretation of the Bible continued to be the constant and paramount, I might almost say the sole object of his thoughts and love. "Before translating the Scriptures from the Hebrew," says Tillemont, "he had produced an edition in Latin very carefully corrected from the Septuagint, not from the general edition into which a quantity of faults had crept, but from that in Origen's Hexapla, which was far more correct and which was sung in the Palestine Churches."[1] Unfortunately the greater part of this translation disappeared during the lifetime of the author. "Pleraque prioris laboris fraude cujusdam amisimus," he wrote to St Augustine.[2] The Psalter, translated as we remember at the instance of Pope Damasus, the book of Job dedicated to Paula and Eustochium, and the prologues to the books of Solomon and of Chronicles, are all that remain of the Hieronymian version of the Septuagint. Another more important and lasting work, however, has consoled the Christian world for this loss, and

[1] Memoirs, etc., St Jerome. Art. liii.   [2] Epist. cxxxiv.

cast an almost unequalled glory upon Jerome's name. To put a stop to the divergencies of the Scriptural versions used in the different Churches and to arrest the mocking criticism of the Jews, who sometimes accused the Christians of quoting the Bible without understanding it, Jerome resolved to translate the Holy Writ from the original. He did not bind himself in this to follow the order of the Canon, and began by the books of Kings, to which he wrote a famous preface which has been the cause of lengthy controversies.

Doubting the deuterocanonical writings of the Old Testament to have been inspired—upon this point the Church has not ratified the learned exegete's uncertainty—Jerome only enumerated the twenty-two canonical books of the Hebrews in his Preface, which he intended to act as a sort of shield and defence to his whole translation of the Bible. "Quasi Galeatum principium," he said; from thence the name of Prologus Galeatus which it has preserved. Jerome wrote this preface about the year 391, and later in 393, sending the first fruits of his labour to Pammachius, he apprised him that he had translated the Sixteen Prophets from Hebrew into Latin. "Borrow," he wrote, "this work from thy cousin Marcella, read the same book in Greek and in Latin, compare with my new version the one I made from the Septuagint, and thou wilt clearly see what difference there is between falsehood and the truth."[1]

We know that Jerome translated the book of Job, and especially Daniel, at the cost of infinite labour.

[1] Epist. xlix. ad Pammachium, 14.

In 394 he translated Esdras and Nehemiah, which he dedicated to Domnion and Rogatus, and the following year he presented his translation of the Chronicles to Chromatius. Shall we enumerate all the other Scriptural works which emanated from the fruitful solitude of Bethlehem? At the request of the monk Sophronius, Jerome translated the Psalms from the Hebrew and, while recovering from a long illness, the Proverbs, Ecclesiastes, and the Song of Solomon. He also commentated the Prophets.

We have selected for quotation a page from the Commentary upon Sophonias, the prophet in whom we seem to hear already a sort of prelude of the *Dies Iræ*.[1] In the downfall of Jerusalem and in the dispersion of the Jews, Jerome shows us the fulfilment of the divine warning. "The day that Jerusalem was taken and destroyed by the Romans, we see a mourning people, decrepit women crowding together, ragged old men bent under the burden of their years and bearing upon their persons and their raiment the impress of the divine wrath. This wretched flock herds together at the spot where rose the cross of our Lord, at the very scene of His glorious resurrection. The standard of the Cross glitters upon the Mount of Olives, while this unhappy race weeps over the ruins of its Temple, without, however, exciting pity. The tears continue to stream down their cheeks, their arms are livid, their locks in wild disorder, and the Roman soldier tries to exact money from them so that they may weep the more. What witness of this scene could say that

[1] Commentar. in Sophoniam (Zephaniah). Lib. i., cap. v. 15, 16.

this was not truly the day of tribulation and anguish, the day of calamity and darkness, the day of clouds and storms, the day of the last trump and of terror? In the midst of their mourning they hear the music of the clarions, and according to the prophecy the sound of feasting has been turned into lamentation. Shrieking with grief they pass over the ashes of the sanctuary, of the overthrown altar, through towns but lately fortified, under the towers of the Temple from which they precipitated James the brother of our Lord." As Villemain says, "Jerome interpreted the ancient curses pronounced upon the Jewish race by the distant glow of the conflagrations which were devastating the East."

After enumerating the translations made by the indefatigable ascetic, Tillemont adds, that in spite of the veneration felt for the Septuagint which the Church had always used since the days of the Apostles, the Hieronymian version ended by superseding it. "It is this which forms the basis of our Vulgate, with the exception of the Psalms, which have remained according to the version of the Septuagint, the books which do not exist in Hebrew, such as the book of Wisdom, Ecclesiasticus, Baruch, Maccabees, and some parts of Daniel and Esther. Even in the others there are a few traces of the ancient version unlike St Jerome's."[1]

Jerome did not escape criticism. What genius indeed, especially when success has crowned him with her laurels, will ever be spared it. Jealousy pursued him with iniquitous and offensive accusa-

[1] Memoirs, St Jerome. Art. lvi.

tions. We read that "Greeks came to accuse him of plundering the Greek authors. Latins reproached him for only caring for works done in the East, as if his acknowledged purpose had not been to throw light upon the Gospel and the Bible by observations made in the very spots where the events had taken place, and to bring his native West into the scientific movement of Eastern Christianity";[1] and a suspicious orthodoxy took exception to the works which seemed to introduce dangerous innovations into liturgical usages. Yet Jerome was happy and as peaceful as his restless nature ever allowed him to be. His letters testify to this peace and happiness which he would fain have shared with all his friends in Rome. "We who have already floated so far upon the tide of life," he wrote to Marcella, "we whose bark has been alternately battered by the storm and pierced by hidden reefs, let us hasten to enter port; a port of solitude and wide fields, where we eat black bread, herbs watered by our own hands, and milk, rustic delicacy, for such is our mean but harmless food. Leading such a life, sleep shall not beguile us from prayer nor an overburdened stomach interrupt our studies. In summer the shade of a tree will provide us with shelter, and in winter a bed of leaves under a clement sky afford us a resting-place. In the spring the land is carpeted with flowers, and the chanting of the Psalms makes even sweeter melody than the warbling of the birds. When winter comes with its cold and snow I have no need to buy fuel; thanks to the neighbouring forest, I shall sleep or

[1] Amédée Thierry.—St Jerome, i. 7.

wake in warmth and comfort, and how economically, for although I spend nothing I cannot freeze. Let Rome keep her uproar, let her arenas run with blood, her circus resound with senseless cries, her theatres overflow with lust, and finally, to speak of our friends, may the senate of matrons be daily visited there. Here we think that it is good to devote ourselves to God and put our trust in him, so that when the day comes for us to exchange our poverty for the kingdom of heaven, we shall be able to say, 'What have I desired in Heaven, what have I yearned for on earth, save only Thee, Oh my God.'"[1]

Among the travellers who visited Jerome there is one whom we cannot pass over in silence, for his name evokes the greatest memories of that age. Towards 393 Alypius, whom the Confessions of St Augustine have taught us to know and love, arrived in Palestine, and according to Tillemont, "saw Jerome and spoke to him of St Augustine. . St Augustine already knew something of Jerome through the fame of his works . but this journey of St Alypius drew them much closer, for Jerome began to love St Augustine from what he heard of him from Alypius, and St Augustine, who was extremely desirous of seeing Jerome, found his wish gratified to a certain extent through his complete sympathy of heart and soul with Alypius, which enabled him to see Jerome through the eyes of the former. . "[2] Fabiola and Oceanus also came to Palestine and settled, she in Paula's convent and he in Jerome's monastery.

[1] Epist. xliii., ad Marcellam.   [2] Memoirs, etc. Art. lxi.

It was about the time of the visit of Alypius that Jerome wrote his celebrated letter to Furia, a Roman widow, and a descendant of the Camilli, in which he commended her widowhood entirely consecrated to God and the poor, and laid down certain austere rules of conduct for her.

CHAPTER V

CONTENTIONS—RUFINUS AND ORIGENISM

A LONG and painful ordeal was about to disturb what St Augustine called "the peaceful joy" which Jerome tasted in his work. It arose from the most unexpected quarter, his adversary being no other than Rufinus, with whom he engaged in a fratricidal conflict over the writings of Origen.

Jerome had first met Rufinus at Aquileia, and they had contracted one of those friendships which seem eternal. It was to this friend of his youth, who had left him to visit the Egyptian Thebaides, that Jerome, isolated in the desert of Chalcis, wrote from a bed of sickness: "Oh! if the Lord Jesus Christ would grant that I might suddenly be transported to thy side as was Philip to the minister of Candacia, and Habakkuk to Daniel, how tenderly would I clasp thee in my arms!" He closed this letter with the following words, which subsequent events so cruelly belied: "I beseech thee, let not thy heart lose sight, as have thine eyes, of a friend so long sought, with such difficulty found, and so hard to retain! Let others gloat over their gold! Friendship is an incomparable possession, a priceless treasure, but the friendship which can perish has never been a true one."[1]

[1] Epist. iii. ad Rufinum monachum.

This last is a somewhat bold assertion, and one which fails to take into account the inconstancy of the human heart, which is liable to take back what it once gave in all sincerity. St Augustine, who was the most devoted and faithful of friends, the mere mention of whose name recalls those of so many beings dear to him whose lives were inseparably interwoven with his own, in speaking of this rupture between Rufinus and Jerome has deplored in touching accents the frailty which undermines or menaces our affections. "What hearts will hereafter dare open themselves to one another; is there any friend to whom one may freely unbosom oneself; where is the friend one does not fear some day to count an enemy, if this rupture which we deplore could have taken place between Jerome and Rufinus? Oh! wretched plight of mankind, and worthy of pity! How can we put faith in what we see in our friend's souls when we cannot foresee what may change them? Yet why lament thus over others when we do not know what we may be ourselves? Man barely and imperfectly knows what he is to-day, he has no conception of what he may be to-morrow."[1]

A friendship worthy of the name and capable of lasting undoubtedly has taxes which levity or selfishness frequently shun. Certain circumstances are favourable to it, create and foster it, and it has often been noticed how great a bond it is for two men to have been born at the same point of time and space, if I may so express it. In the course of years contemporaries, even those who differ most in thought,

[1] Epist. cx. inter Epist. Hieronymi, 6.

are drawn together and sometimes end in agreeing, seeming to feel nearer one another than they do to the newer generation, who, making no distinctions, are equally contemptuous or disdainful of them. How much easier then is a friendship like that of Rufinus and Jerome, built not only upon a common origin and memories but upon mutual tastes, studies and beliefs. As Augustine reminded the latter, they had both grown to manhood unfettered by the world, nourished upon the precious words of the Scriptures, and dwelling in Palestine, where an echo of the Lord's words proclaiming peace linger in the traces of his footsteps. It was not at this age when usually sentiments as well as thoughts take firmer root in the soul, and life shapes its future course, that the friendship between Rufinus and Jerome should have been severed had it not always contained the seeds of death. But from the very first it had been founded upon a mistake; for Rufinus and Jerome, who had thought that they thoroughly understood each other, were in reality separated by profound and irreducible differences. Studious and learned but narrow-minded and contemptuous of anything of which he was ignorant, ever ready to introduce a sophistical skill and a cutting irony into polemical discussions, Rufinus was totally unlike Jerome, whose ardent soul sought the truth under every form, and who seemed more capable of violence than of bitterness. We must acknowledge that at times Jerome, yielding to this spirit of violence, gave vent to strangely intemperate language, of which vivid examples may be found in many of his letters, in his apology against

Rufinus, and even in his Scriptural works, where one would expect to find only the serene inspiration which emanates from God. A famous writing of Origen's gave rise to a stormy quarrel and an irrevocable rupture between the two friends. It was curious that the timid writer, who took exception to the most legitimate of Jerome's innovations and behind whose watchful orthodoxy lurked a conservative and moody spirit of distrust, should have been the champion of the brilliant and audacious Alexandrian, who seems to us one of the most dazzling and in certain respects one of the most sympathetic personalities of the Christian school of Alexandria. When a child he had wished to be reunited to his father, Leonidas, through martyrdom; when a man he continued in the Didascalia the teaching introduced by Pantenus and Clement; and in his old age he was privileged to suffer for the truth. He patiently and unshrinkingly examined every branch of sacred lore. As a critic he undertook prodigious works upon the Greek versions of the Bible; as an apologist he responded with a vigour and point which have not suffered by age to the mocking strictures of Celsus, and as a thinker he broached the most abstruse points of Christian dogmatism; but unfortunately the soundness of Origen's views as a theologian fell short of those he held as a critic and apologist, which was the cause of the wide-spread controversies he occasioned. Even during his lifetime the audacity of his views attracted attention, and we are told by a writer, always seeking to gather any proof in ecclesiastical history of the vigilance and far-reaching intervention of the Roman Pontiffs, that "towards the end of his life he found himself obliged to justify himself to Pope Fabian and to retract certain propositions."[1] Origen was especially censured after his death; he was blamed for his views upon the pre-existence of souls and upon the successive ordeals which in his mind replaced the dogma of the irrevocable and final sanction of the human life, and upon the future resurrection which he seems to have spiritualised to the point of robbing this dogma of its obvious and traditional meaning. He was considered by some a precursor of Arius. He was opposed by Saints such as Methodius, Bishop of Olympia in Lycia, Peter, Bishop of Alexandria, and Eustathius, Bishop of Antioch; but on the other hand illustrious disciples and intrepid champions of his cause rose from the ranks of orthodoxy. St Gregory Thaumaturgus, whom he had baptized, glorified him in touching terms, Pamphilus the holy martyr wrote his apology, while St Gregory of Nyssa and Didymus of Alexandria considered him their master.

We do not assert, as did Rufinus to justify the veneration which clung so long to Origen's memory, that he was never guilty of the errors attributed to him and that the heretics inserted them into the "Periarchon" (the Book on the Fundamental Doctrines); neither do we try to put a favourable interpretation upon its most unorthodox tenets. It is enough to repeat the judicious words of Mgr.

[1] Duchesne, "Ecclesiastical autonomies," ehap. iv.—The Roman Church before Constantine.

Freppel: "The author of the 'Periarchon' did not at any period of his life put himself in opposition to the Church's teachings, which always represented to him the infallible rule of Faith. Firm in his principles he could only have erred in the application by mistaking for liberal opinions what really was contrary to the Catholic dogma. Origen believed it possible safely to construct a philosophical system founded upon the Revelation, the principal idea of which was taken from Plato. However, he only formulated this system with many reservations, as a sort of hypothesis and as a mere mental exercise."[1]

But to return to Rufinus and Jerome, can one wonder that two youths, enthusiastically interested as they were in learning, should have plunged with ecstasy into the spring of knowledge which Origen made accessible to them; can one wonder that Jerome should have proclaimed him "the Master of the Churches after the Apostles?"[2] Yet much as he admired Origen's learning and genius, Jerome was careful to refrain from "Origenism." In his commentary on the Epistle to the Ephesians he confuted the error of the pre-existence of souls. He was able to write: "I have praised Origen as an interpreter, not as a dogmatising theologian."[3] During the years of whose history we are about to give an outline, he was becoming disillusioned of the master whom he had so admired, and when

[1] Origen, 37th Lesson.
[2] Lib. de nominibus hebraicis. Præfat.
[3] Epist. lxxxiv. ad Pammachium, 2.

in 394 a monk called Aterbius came to Jerusalem and denounced the Origenists in his diocese, Rufinus especially, to the Bishop John, Jerome had no hesitation in publicly denying the errors which were also imputed to him. This, however, was only a preliminary campaign against Origenism and those suspected of it, the real war was opened by St Epiphanius of Salamis, whom our readers already know, having seen him as Paula's guest in Rome, and at Cyprus where he returned her hospitality. The virtues and works of Epiphanius were the object of a legitimate and well-merited admiration. "This aged man," says Amédée Thierry, who cannot be accused of being over-indulgent in his judgments of the saints, "gave proof of his heroism when, consuming his life in the search of heresies, braving hunger and thirst and the ill-treatment of man, even penetrating into the heart of the Arabian deserts to study the deviations of the Christian Faith, he firmly upheld the chain of Apostolic tradition which in the East is so easily weakened by imagination and fancy."[1] It is not, however, disrespectful to the holy Pontiff to acknowledge that he was at times carried away by excess of zeal. The line of conduct which, without any regard to the rights of John Chrysostom, Epiphanius pursued at Constantinople towards the close of a life which covered nearly a hundred years, can only be explained by the blind confidence he put in the perverted guidance of Theophilus of Alexandria, and can only be justified by the un-

[1] St John Chrysostom and the Empress Eudoxia. Book III., iii.

deniable good faith of a soul which everywhere waged a truceless war against heresy. Upon the Episcopal throne of Jerusalem Epiphanius found less exalted virtues and doctrines less sound than those he later so unfortunately misjudged at Constantinople. We fear that in junctures like these he did not display all the prudence and tact desirable. Respectfully welcomed by the clergy and inhabitants of the Holy City, he denounced Origen in a speech in which the Bishop John thought he detected allusions personal to himself. The Bishop of Jerusalem, stung by this attack, created a diversion by scoffing at the coarse anthropomorphism in which certain adversaries of Origen, fearing his refined spiritualism, sought an illusory refuge. Epiphanius retorted: "All that John, through the union of priesthood my brother, and by reason of his youth my son, has just said against the heresy of the Anthropomorphites I consider well spoken and much to the purpose, but as we both condemn the Anthropomorphites, it is but just that we should also both condemn the impious dogmas of Origen."[1] John, however, refused to make the complete and sudden disavowal for which he was asked. On another occasion when John had resumed his catechetical teaching in the presence of Epiphanius, the latter, according to St Jerome, abruptly left Jerusalem, and as if alarmed at the discourses he had heard there fled to the monastery at Bethlehem, where he evinced his grief at having communicated with a heretical bishop. Jerome and

[1] Tillemont.—Memoirs, etc., St Jerome. Art. lxvi.

his monks, foreseeing the results of such an outburst, entreated Epiphanius to return to John and if possible to effect a reconciliation; and the Bishop of Salamis, apparently yielding to their prayers, returned to Jerusalem. However, he only passed through the town, arriving in the evening and leaving during the night for the convent of Vieil-Ad, which he had founded and formerly governed, and which was in the diocese of Eleutheropolis. From thence he wrote to John urging him to condemn Origen, and to all the monasteries in Palestine exhorting them to cease all relations with the Bishop of Jerusalem should he not give satisfaction on the subject of his faith.

Hostilities now broke out between John and Epiphanius, and between those who, like Rufinus and Melania, remained faithful to the Bishop of Jerusalem, and the monks at Bethlehem who considered him an abettor of heresy. Jerome deemed it sufficient to keep upon terms with Gelasius of Cæsarea, the Metropolitan of Palestine. Would it be casting a slur on the memory of the illustrious hermit to repeat Tillemont's severe words? "He had cut himself off from communion with his bishop, against whom nothing had been proved but a mere suspicion founded on the accusation of St Epiphanius, who, saint though he was, was not always judicious in his words and acts. He afterwards behaved towards St John Chrysostom in much the same manner as he had to John of Jerusalem."[1] The animosity of a bishop who was quick to take offence

[1] Memoirs, etc., St Jerome. Art. lxxv.

and who had been deeply wounded, soon made itself felt.

To procure for the monks of Bethlehem the religious ministrations which had been denied them by John's priests, while a pious terror kept Jerome and his friend Vincent from the altar, Epiphanius almost forced Jerome's brother Paulinian, whose youth was to the Bishop of Jerusalem an additional though not the most important grievance, to be ordained. Although the ordination had taken place at Vieil-Ad, over which place John could not claim any authority, he regarded it as an outrage, and resorted to anathema as a means of revenge. Jerome, in his eloquent and indignant defence, which is not conspicuous for its respect, gives an account of the harshness with which his friends were treated. "Do we rend the Church," he asks the Bishop of Jerusalem in defiant tones, "we whose convent of Bethlehem is in communion with the Church? Is it not rather thou, whose faith may be sound but is disguised through pride? Or perhaps thy faith is perverted; then art thou the real disturber of the peace. What! we rend the Church, we who, a few months ago on Whitsunday, when the sun was obscured and the trembling world thought that the Supreme Judge was about to appear amongst us (an allusion to the strange phenomena which terrified the East in 396), presented forty persons of all ages and both sexes to your priest for baptism, in spite of there being five priests in our monastery who had the right to baptise, but who were unwilling to do ought which might offend thee, for fear of furnishing thee with an excuse for persisting in a silence which is injurious to the true faith. Is it not rather thou who rendest the Church? Thou who at Easter forbade the priest to baptise our catechumens? We were obliged to send them to Diospolis (Lydda), where Dionysius, bishop and confessor, initiated them into Christianity. We rend the Church, we who outside of our cells do not claim in it the least place! Is it not rather thou who agitatest her, thou who refusest admission into her fold to anyone recognising as a priest Paulinian, whom Epiphanius ordained? Since that moment we gaze from afar upon the Sepulchre of our Lord, groaning at being banished from the holy spot to which even heretics have access." " So it is we," pursues Jerome, giving way to indignation, " who rend the Church, and not thou who didst refuse a shelter to the living and a sepulchre to the dead, and who didst scheme for the exile of thy brethren. Who excited against us, thereby endangering our lives, the awful monster who threatened the entire world? Who has left until this very day the bones and innocent ashes of the Saints to the mercy of wind and rain? It is by these gentle means that the good shepherd bids us make peace, and reproaches us for wishing to construct an independent government, we who are united in communion and charity with every bishop professing the true faith! . ."[1]

This long extract shows us the motives which inspired Jerome's actions, the manner in which he justified them in his own eyes, and the passionate

[1] Contra Joannem Hierosolomytanum ad Pammachium. Lib. 42, 43.

turmoil of his soul. It also discloses the means to which the Bishop of Jerusalem resorted to rid himself of his fiery opponent: he had procured an order of banishment from Rufinus, the sinister Præfect of the Prætorium, and its execution was only arrested by the tragic death of this powerful favourite. Jerome continued to dwell in Bethlehem.

Attempts were made to bring about a reconciliation between the bishop and the hermit, but the intervention of Archelaus, the governor of Palestine, a man, according to Jerome, of great eloquence, and eminently a Christian, proved fruitless. John seems to have taken pains to discourage him by making interminable delays out of the most trivial causes. In point of fact he wished to refer to another judgment, to that of the governor of the province, and claimed that which was his due, the intervention of a bishop. But he sought, not in Palestine nor in the patriarchate of the East, but in Egypt, this ecclesiastical arbitration which he claimed as his right. "You who seek to follow the rules of the Church," said Jerome, "and invoke the canons of the Nicean Council, pray tell me what has the Bishop of Alexandria to do with Palestine? If I mistake not, the decree of Nicea was to the effect that Cæsarea should be the metropolis of Palestine, and Antioch that of the entire East. Therefore it was to the Bishop of Cæsarea that you should have taken this matter, or if you wished to seek further a-field for a judge, you should have written to the Bishop of Antioch."[1]

[1] Contra Joanem Hierosolomytanum. Lib. 37.

The Bishop of Jerusalem had had his own reasons for addressing himself to the Patriarch of Alexandria. Theophilus, who was the head of that branch of the Church which still gloried in Origen, in spite of the dissension he had certainly created in it, had long been an admirer of the great Alexandrian, and as there was nothing at that time to predict that he was soon to become the ardent promoter of a reactionary movement, and that his enmity, inspired by hatred, would persecute, and accuse of Origenism, the venerable monks known as Long Brothers, and their protector, St John Chrysostom, the Bishop of Jerusalem counted upon finding in him a favourable judge ; and, in fact, his representative in Palestine, the priest Isidorus, was won over to his cause beforehand. All attempt at a reconciliation completely failed, and the two adversaries continued to plead their respective causes before the Church.

While this internecine war was dragging its weary course another had broken out, for Theodosius on his death had left the Empire, which he had known how to govern and defend, in weak hands; Alaric and his Goths devastated Thrace and Greece, and an incursion of Huns invaded the East. Jerome has described in many passages the anguish and sorrow of those terrible days. " Last year " (that is in 398), he wrote to Heliodorus, " the wolves, not of Arabia (which are mentioned in Scripture), but the wolves of the north which have overrun so many provinces in so short a time, came forth from the confines of the Caucasus and precipitated themselves upon us. How many monasteries they sacked ! how many rivers ran with blood! Antioch and all the towns situated on the Cydnus, Orontes, and Euphrates were besieged, and captives driven forth like herds of cattle. In their terror Arabia, Phœnicia, Palestine, and Egypt imagined themselves already captive."[1] In another letter he writes: "May the Lord Jesus remove from the Roman Empire these devouring beasts, which arrive unexpectedly, more swift than rumour. Neither religion, nor dignity, nor age find mercy at the hands of the barbarians; they have no pity upon the babe in its cradle."[2] Upon a report which was spread abroad that the Huns would march straight upon Jerusalem, attracted by the treasures which the devotion of the Christian world had amassed there, Jerome hastily procured some vessels to transport his monks, and the nuns of Paula's convents, to a place of safety. Encamped upon the shores of the Mediterranean the fugitives only awaited the first tidings of the invader's arrival to embark. The sea was stormy, the winds tempestuous, but as Jerome said, giving expression to the mortal anguish which chastity or pity inspired in so many souls, "I feared shipwreck less than I did the barbarians, and had less horror of our loss at sea than of the dishonour of our virgins."[3] The enemy, however, never came, and Jerome and Paula returned to Bethlehem, whither their former pious duties recalled them. But the widow Fabiola, who had joined them in Palestine and who had followed them to the coast, refused to return to such an unprotected

---

[1] Epist. lx. ad Heliodorum. Epitaphium Nepotiani, 16.
[2] Epist. lxxvii. ad Oceanum, 8. [3] Epist. lxxvii. 8.

wilderness, and returned in voluntary poverty to Italy, where she had once lived in opulence.

In the funeral oration of the priest Nepotian, from which we extract this tragic account, Jerome wrote: "At that time there were dissensions in our midst, and before the scandal of our domestic quarrels the invasions of the barbarians sank into insignificance." How often in the most troublous times, men under the menace or the blow of calamity, have persisted in private contentions or in scientific controversies, which distract their attention from the sight of the universal misery. Can one wonder at this? Is not man generally most struck by what he hears or sees in his immediate surroundings, and are not the interests and ideas to which he has devoted his life the object of his principal and most constant preoccupation? Does it seem strange or wrong that Jerome should have continued to wage his ceaseless war against Origenism and other errors, in the midst of all the sorrow and horror of those disastrous days. No doubt unworthy sentiments may sometimes have mingled with the lofty motives which actuated him; he may have been mistaken in his judgments and given vent to undue violence in his language; but what, however, remains an undeniable fact is, that the Hermit of Bethlehem desired before everything the triumph of Truth, which at all times deserves to triumph, and should ever be defended. It was this which occasioned the struggles which Jerome, and later Augustine, Leo the Great, Gregory the Great, and so many illustrious doctors of the Church maintained against heresy, amid evils so desperate that they seemed to herald the approaching end of the world. These great men excelled in the saving and the encouragement of stricken but shrinking souls, but they did not forget that Eternal Truth is the primary blessing and the supreme refuge of every soul, and without allowing themselves to be discouraged or turned from their purpose they continued to proclaim its imprescriptible rights.

Isidorus the priest, after a repulse which was but too clearly foreseen, returned to Alexandria in 396. Theophilus came himself to Jerusalem, but his sympathies were entirely with John and his censure for Jerome. "You advise me to observe the canons of the Church," wrote Jerome; "I thank you for this warning, for 'Whom the Lord loveth He chasteneth, and scourgeth every son whom He receiveth.'[1] Know this, however, nothing is nearer to my heart than to keep the law of Christ, not to exceed the limits imposed by the Fathers, and never to forget the Roman Faith, which is eulogised by the Apostle, and which it is the glory of the Alexandrian Church to share."[2]

The reconciliation, however, took place. The Patriarch of Alexandria, who had hitherto defended Origen, changed his opinions. "Did he realise in a sudden illumination of the conscience," asks Thierry, "that Origen, who was very excellent and useful in the hands of the learned, presented a real danger to the ignorant? Did he see that the needs of the soul are not the same for everyone, and that a far-seeing priest should remove from the pathway of the simple

[1] Hebrews xii. 6. [2] Epist. lxiii. ad Theophilum, 2.

the stumbling block which the philosopher or the theologian would avoid?"[1] It is possible that he did, for Theophilus united a thorough knowledge of men to his theological science, yet there are other and less praiseworthy motives which account for this change in his conduct. It was entirely to the interest of the persecutor of the monks known as Long Brothers, to the jealous and passionate adversary of St John Chrysostom, henceforth to regard the Origenism imputed to his enemies as a most pernicious heresy. From that moment Epiphanius and Jerome, who were antagonistic to Origen's doctrines, became dear to the patriarch and were treated by him as partisans. John of Jerusalem, who was an indifferent theologian and who, moreover, preferred the authority of the Patriarch of Alexandria to the nearer and more inconvenient supervision of the Metropolitan of Cæsarea, followed, or at least did not thwart the former in his evolution, and removed all the interdictions which had been laid upon the monks at Bethlehem. Rufinus, fired by the example of his bishop, made some advances towards Jerome, and they were both reconciled in the Church of the Resurrection at Jerusalem, where together they partook of the Holy Sacrament. This was in 397.

Jerome's reconciliation with John was sincere. "I think," said Tillemont, "that Jerome will not be found to have said anything, after this animated quarrel was over, that could have injured the bishop's reputation."[2] John, however, at the time

[1] St Jerome. Book viii.
[2] Memoirs, etc., St Jerome. Art. lxxxi.

of the Pelagian controversy, displayed the same faults of character which he had shown in the Origenist controversies, and through a culpable inaction which strangely resembled complicity, identified himself with the persecutors of the hermit. A fierce and inexorable war broke out afresh between Jerome and Rufinus, but before retailing its painful incidents let us draw attention to the aggression to which Jerome was subjected by Vigilantius (a Spaniard in whom Paulinian had been deceived when he commended him to Jerome), and also of Jerome's answer to it. Vigilantius accused Jerome of Origenism, alleging the extracts which the hermit had taken from the works of the great Alexandrian. Further, and it is for this that this forerunner of the heretical leaders of the sixteenth century is best known and that he most deserved Jerome's condemnations, Vigilantius rejected the invocation of the Saints, the cult of relics, the prayers for the dead, the practice of fasting, and the celibacy of priests and monks. Jerome had no difficulty in refuting the accusation of Origenism, but he was better employed than in his own defence. With a logical eloquence and force which did not shrink from personalities, he also refuted the objections of Vigilantius, and put in their proper light the sacred and historical character of the dogmas and usages, against which the audacious innovator was rebelling.

Heliodorus, a friend of Jerome's and for some time a companion in his travels, had an unusually gifted nephew called Nepotianus. At the beginning of his career he had been engaged in the Emperor's service, and, having set the same example to the court of Theodosius whieh in after years Francis Borgia and Louis of Gonzaga were to give to the courts of Charles V. and Philip II., he renounced a world which had never given him any cause for disillusionment and consecrated himself to the ministry of the altar. Jerome on this occasion wrote him a famous letter in which he enumerated the austere duties of the sacerdotal life. Amongst many other lessons to be found in it is the following, which applies to all preachers, and which Fenelon has inserted in his third " Dialogue upon Eloquence " : "When teaching in the church do not excite the applause but rather the lamentations of the people ; let the tears of your auditors be your commendation. The sermons of a priest should overflow with Holy Scripture. Be not an orator, but a sincere expounder of the mysteries of your God."[1] This letter was written in 394 ; a few years later, in 396, this young man, whom Heliodorus had vainly counted on as a successor to his Episcopal See of Attino, was smitten by death; and Jerome in an eloquent letter, while lamenting the friend he was losing, strove to console the friend who still remained. In it he depicted the serene death of the youthful priest, and in a delicate and touching passage reminded him that the last thoughts of the dying man had been turned towards him. "His face wore a look of joy; amid the tearful onlookers he alone smiled . you would have thought, not that he was dying, but that he was about to start for a long journey; not that he was

[1] Epist. lii. ad Nepotianum, 8.

leaving his friends, but that he was going to find others. Who would believe that at this supreme moment he should have remembered our friendship, and that his soul should have been sensible to the sweetness of our mutual affection, even in the throes of death? Having taken his uncle's hand, he said: Send this vestment which I wore in Christ's service to my beloved father in years, my brother by the union of priesthood, and all the affection due to your nephew expend on him whom, with me, you already love."[1] This funeral oration, for such it really is, which is a precursor of many later masterpieces of Christian eloquence, contains, as we have already said, a vivid picture of the evils which were then devastating the world, and closes with a reference to the vanity and frailty of things human. "Let us rouse ourselves. Do you know the instant in which you passed from childhood to youth, from youth to man's estate, and finally to old age? Each day brings death and change to us, and yet we believe ourselves to be immortal. Even what I am dictating, what is being written, and what I shall re-read, is so much cut off from my life. We write and write again; our letters cross the seas, the vessels plough through the waves, and each wave carries with it an instant of our life. . ." The Christian, the priest, however, does not dwell long upon these melancholy thoughts, but turns his gaze to higher things. "Our only blessing," Jerome continues, "is our union with Christ and our union with one another in the charity of Christ. . . . Charity is undying; it lives eternally in

[1] Epist. lx. ad Heliodorum. Epitaphium Nepotiani, 13.

the hearts of men; through it Nepotianus, although departed, is still with us, and, across the space which divides us, still clasps our hands in his."[1]

We cannot linger over these touching pages for we must return to the Origenist quarrel, which again sprang into life and distracted Jerome from his work, I might almost say from his sorrow. Rufinus started for Rome, and on arriving in the Eternal City he met a man called Macarus, a man of the world "distinguished," he says, "by his faith, his nobility, and his life,"[2] who was occupied at the time in defending in a special treatise, the dogma of the divine providence against the fatalistic error and misleading fancies of astrology. The difficulties of such an abstruse subject frequently brought him to a standstill, but firmly believing in a dream, he expected someone who would soon give him its solution. He believed Rufinus to be the man his dream predicted, for could not Rufinus, who had just returned from Palestine, who was familiar with Christian literature in the East, and who knew Origen, whose fame had penetrated into the Latin world so thoroughly, could not he initiate Macarus, probably an ignorant, or at least indifferent scholar of Greek, into the works of the celebrated Alexandrian, and thus allow him to draw from his vast wells of thought. Rufinus also believed that he was the man, and translated for his friend first the Apology of Origen by the holy martyr Pamphilus, and afterwards the Periarchon (the book of Fundamental Doctrines).

[1] Epist. lx. 19. [2] Rufini Apologiæ. Lib. i. 11.

This last undertaking entailed considerable risk, for of all Origen's work none had awakened so much distrust or called forth the censure of orthodoxy more than the Periarchon. Rufinus was fully aware of this, and he owns that he only presented an expurgated copy to the Latins, in which extracts from other works of Origen explained and completed the obscure passages. "One cannot deny," says Mgr. Freppel, "that Rufinus exceeded his privileges of translator. He remodelled the original text from an entirely personal point of view, and even were it admitted, as in fact we do admit, that he has rightly grasped Origen's thoughts upon the question of the Trinity, he should not have presumed to recast any part whatsoever of the work."[1] In the preface to his translation Rufinus, to justify his temerity, cited the example given by St Jerome, for although he does not actually name him, his manner of praising him, and the mention of the works which the Hermit of Bethlehem had already translated, sufficiently indicate whom he meant. Rufinus declared that he was following in the footsteps of one greater than himself. If Jerome sometimes corrected the Book of Fundamental Doctrines, was he not the first to suppress or modify anything in his version of the Homilies of Origen at which the austere orthodoxy of the Latins might take exception? Through a bold stroke Rufinus gained two points, for on one hand he reinstated Origen, and the Alexandrian, who until then had been under suspicion, returned to Rome, if not victorious at least acquitted; and

[1] Origen. 14th lesson.

on the other, he associated with his cause and with the cause of Origen the man who formerly in Palestine had, with Epiphanius and Theophilus, been his most bitter adversary. In Jerome's eyes, Origenism was at that time the Church's greatest peril. He therefore rejected these compromising eulogies and this detrimental solidarity. Besides, he also thought that it was better to resolutely broach the most unorthodox of the great Alexandrian's works and expose its audacities and errors, than to give the misled Romans a modified and therefore a deceptive version of the Periarchon. He accordingly undertook a complete translation of this work, which, however, is no longer extant. In his correspondence Jerome gives an explanation of his past conduct, of the works in which he had exalted Origen, and the admiration he had evinced for him. The following passage is extracted from a letter written to Oceanus, and to Paula's son-in-law Pammachius. It atones for the injury which Jerome's translation of the malicious pamphlet of Theophilus did to the great man's memory, and it will please those of our own time who, without disputing the errors by which the bold and subtle Alexandrian was led astray, still honour him for his virtues and labours. "If you wish to praise Origen," says Jerome, " praise him as I do. He was great even from childhood, and the true son of a martyr ; he governed the Christian school in Alexandria, where he had succeeded the learned priest Clement; he abhorred licence and trampled upon avarice; he knew the Scriptures by heart, and his days and nights were spent in the study of Holy

Writ. . What one of us could read all that he has written? Who could fail to admire his intense love for the Scriptures? And if some Judas, in bitter zeal, should allege his errors, we will reply boldly: 'Homer becomes at times lethargic. Is it not excusable in a long poem? Let us not copy the errors of one whose virtues we are unable to imitate.'"[1]

In Rome, the translation of Rufinus had greatly excited all who had Jerome's reputation and the cause of orthodoxy at heart. Marcella, the ascetic's learned friend, was among the first to perceive the danger; at first she kept silence through modesty, but as she saw it growing she warned him of it. Rufinus, afraid of the storm which seemed to be gathering, left Rome, and provided by Pope Siricius with credentials, returned to Aquileia. It was under Anastasius, the successor of Siricius, that Origenism received its death blows in the East and in the West. Theophilus prosecuted it in his patriarchate of Alexandria with a zeal tinged with a fierce love of power and an intolerance of all contradiction. He even pretended to discover it among the monks of Nitria, guilty of having defended the good cause, and in John Chrysostom their protector. Jerome joined in this campaign by translating the synodical letters of Theophilus, and possibly even an odious pamphlet whose authorship Facundus of Hermione, an author of the sixth century, attributes to the Patriarch. "It is more," wrote Tillemont, "than for his honour we could wish to believe."[2] Jerome, however, joined

---

[1] Epist. lxxxiv., Pammachio et Oceano, 8.
[2] Memoirs, etc., St Jerome. Art. xcviii.

in this contention with unquestionable sincerity, for Theophilus, whom he only saw from afar, seemed to him an intrepid champion of the faith. In 400, a Roman Council, the Acts of which have been lost, condemned the Errors of Origen.

The Confession of Faith which Rufinus sent to Pope Anastasius was completely orthodox, and there is nothing to prove that the censure of Anastasius was directed against him any more than against all those who had propagated erroneous or dangerous books. The friendship of venerable personages like St Paulinus of Nola, St Chromatius of Aquileia, and St Gaudentius of Brescia, which Rufinus always retained, testify to the purity of his faith. Rufinus was over bold, he let loose a whirlwind in which his reputation nearly perished, but he was never heretical.

Did his charity, as well as his faith, emerge intact from these painful conflicts? Anyone who has read his Apology, his "Invectives against Jerome," for such is the name which has clung to this work, can only answer in the negative. "He devoted three years to this work," says Amédée Thierry, "which appeared fragment by fragment; he divided it into two books to which he later added a supplement. He had a double aim, first to exonerate himself from the crime of heresy by casting upon Jerome the accusation directed towards himself, and then to dishonour Jerome and to throw odium on his name by personal imputations, lamenting the while being forced to such measures."[1] Indeed no pamphlet

[1] St Jerome. Lib. iv.

has ever been composed with more cunning hatred, nor has ever struck the adversary more surely. It was the man whom Rufinus aimed at in the writer. We will not linger over the Origenism of which Jerome was accused, greatly on the strength of extracts from his own writings. Why should not Jerome have shared the privilege common to all authors of explaining, and if necessary of retracting, his former writings? He certainly cannot be accused of having been actuated by personal interest; the mistake which he made, if indeed it was a mistake, was in contradicting himself. The venom of Rufinus sought other outlets. According to him, Jerome was the enemy of mankind; a traducer of the faithful, whose customs he had calumniated in his book upon Virginity, at the risk of justifying and even magnifying the calumnies of the pagans; a traducer of the works of Ambrose, the great bishop; a traducer of Rome, the capital of the Christian world; and a traducer of all authors, either Greek or Latin, who had preceded him. One grievance which Rufinus put forward with malignant insistence, was the important part the pagan authors played in Jerome's works and in his thoughts. In vain had Jerome after a famous vision sworn never to reopen any secular book. "Peruse his writings and see if there is a single page which does not point to his having again become a Ciceronian, and in which he does not speak of 'Our Cicero,' 'Our Homer,' 'Our Virgil'; he even boasts of having read the works of Pythagoras, which according to the erudite are no longer in existence. In almost all his works quotations from secular authors are far more numerous and lengthy than those from the Prophets and Apostles. Even when writing to women or maidens, who in our holy books seek only subjects for edification, he intersperses his letters with quotations from Horace, Cicero or Virgil." [1]

He was guilty of a still graver offence. "In the monastery at Bethlehem Jerome performed the office of grammarian, and he expounded Virgil, the humourists, cynics, and historians, to children who had been confided to him to be inspired with the fear of God." [2] The hermit, enamoured as he was of pagan law, had recourse to the erudition of the Hebrew doctors to assist him in his biblical works; he preferred these masters to any others because "they alone preserved the truth of the Scriptures." Rufinus was certainly not wanting in learning, yet partly through his violent antipathy to Jerome, partly through mental cowardice, this strange champion of Origen took the side of routine and ignorance against the ascetic. The smallest change introduced by Jerome into the accepted translations of the sacred works, for example the substitution of one word for another, roused the indignation of Rufinus. "Now that the world is waxing old and all things are drawing near their end," he exclaimed, " let us write upon the tombs of the Ancients " (the touchingly symbolic picture of Jonas asleep was frequently reproduced upon these tombs), "let us write so as to inform those who have not read it in their Bibles that Jonas reposed in the shade of an ivy, and not in the shade

[1] Apol. Lib. sec. 7.   [2] *Ibid.*, 8.

of a gourd."[1] He was sometimes very crafty in his criticisms, for example, when he reproached Jerome with the doubts which it was well known that he entertained of the canonicity of several portions of the Book of Daniel. In the next breath, however, placing the legends which vainly aspire to be called traditions upon the same footing as the dogmatic traditions of the Church, Rufinus condemned as a crime Jerome's rejection of the fable of the seventy-two old men who, detained by order of Ptolemy Philadelphus, King of Egypt, each in a separate cell, came forth with an identical version of the Bible.[2] On more than one occasion and under various forms he put this question, with which men have often tried to discourage the apostles of the most legitimate movements: "who of all the great men, your predecessors, dare embark upon the work which you have undertaken?"[3]

The pamphlet of Rufinus which was brought to Jerome by his brother Paulinian, demanded an answer. It was surely the hermit's right, his duty even, to refute accusations which defamed both his character and his works. He accordingly answered his adversary's "Invectives" by an "Apology," and Thierry tells us that Jerome was never more inspired than in these pages, which contain theological discussions, self-justification, denouncement of the enemy, lamentations, and finally, anger, when his indignation overcame him. The trenchancy of his style, the flow of language, the force of argument, all were indeed marvellous. The "Apology"

[1] Apol. Lib. sec. 35.   [2] *Ibid.*, 33.   [3] Apol. Lib. ii. 32.

of Rufinus doubtless bears the stamp of great talent, but Jerome's that of genius. We must acknowledge that Jerome's wrath, which was justifiable when restrained within due limits, vented itself in regrettable personalities.

Several years later, in a letter to Rusticus describing the happiness of a monastic life, and full of the most affectingly tender passages, Jerome sketched a picture worthy of the humourist and the satirist, Plautus and Juvenal, whose works he was reproached for reading, but which he probably knew by heart. He dubbed this picture "Grunnius," and it has never been denied that it was Rufinus he strove to portray. At the time of this letter, which dates from 408, the aged athlete was not yet disabled, and a passage of his commentary upon Ezekiel, written after the death of Rufinus, seems to prove that he never became so. It is true that other saints have left a reputation of greater gentleness and clemency than did the Hermit of Bethlehem. Let us recall the words of Pope Sixtus V. who, passing one day before a picture representing Jerome in the act of striking his breast with a stone, cried: "You do well to hold that pebble in your hand, for without it the Church would never have canonised you."

Rufinus, driven from Aquileia by the invasion of the Goths, retired to Sicily, where he pursued his labours of history and translation until his death there in 410.

CHAPTER VI

JOYS AND SORROWS—JEROME AS MENTOR

WE have at last come to the end of the quarrel which, after agitating the life of the hermit, has left a painful impression even upon posterity. St Jerome's controversy with St Augustine, which will shortly be mentioned, was never as impassioned as his dispute with Rufinus, and ended in the interchange of mutual proofs of esteem, sympathy and respect between the theologian of Hippo and the aged writer.

The close of the fourth century was a period of mourning for Jerome. Paula's second daughter, Paulina, died in 397, but it was not until two years later that Jerome wrote to Pammachius, her bereaved husband, a letter which was both a letter of condolence and a funeral oration. He called himself a tardy consoler (*serus consolator*), without, however, giving any explanation for his delay. In this letter, which ends with the touching passage quoted below, he paid tribute not only to the departed Christian, but also to Paula, Eustochium and Pammachius. . . "In concluding," he said, "I perceive that Blesilla is missing from your group and from my portrayal of it. I have almost forgotten to mention her who has gone before you to her God. From five you are reduced to three, for two have been ravished by death. Blesilla and her sister Paulina sleep the sleep of peace, and you who survive them, standing between their graves, will soar to Christ on a lighter wing."[1]

The date of a letter which Jerome wrote to Leta, the wife of Paula's son, Toxotius, may be placed somewhere between 398 and 400. Leta, who had more than once been disappointed in her hopes of maternity, at last gave birth to a daughter, whose existence she believed due to the intercession of a martyr, and whom even before her birth she had dedicated to a religious life. The child was called Paula, after its grandmother. In one respect the family into which Paula was born strongly resembled many of the present day. Leta had sprung, as Jerome reminded her when he wrote "*tu es nata de impari matrimonio*," from a mixed union, for although the daughter of a Christian, the daughter-in-law of a saint, and the wife of Toxotius, whom she had converted to Christianity, her father, Albinus, was a pagan pontiff. To-day, with very rare exceptions, pagans and Christians do not intermarry, but in many families does not the more or less conscious rationalism, the theoretical or merely practical unbelief of the husband, or of the master spirit, remind us of the paganism of Albinus? Jerome describes in touching terms how the polytheist was influenced by the faith of those who surrounded him. "It seems incredible that a grandchild of the pontiff Albinus should have owed its existence to a

[1] Epist. lxvi. ad Pammachium, 15.

vow of its mother's, that it should lisp the Alleluia of the Christ in the presence of its delighted grandfather, and that the aged man should clasp one of God's virgins in his arms. Let us take courage; a pious and faithful household has converted its only infidel member, and Albinus, surrounded by a flock of Christian children and grandchildren, has already become a candidate for baptism."[1]

The child was still in its cradle when Leta and her friend Marcella wrote to Jerome asking him for some suggestions for its education. In certain ways the letter which Jerome sent in answer may be considered a treatise upon the "education of girls," always taking into consideration that it was originally written for a Roman patrician maiden of the fifth century, a child who was dedicated to a religious life by the most earnest vows. Jerome did not wish to deprive Paula of the affection of her family. "May her grandfather," he said, "hold her in his arms, may she know her father by his smile, may she be gentle to all so that her relations may rejoice at having been the stem of such a rose."[2] Yet at the same time he early subjected her to a training, and sketched for her a plan of study, without, however, causing her to neglect the more modest tasks inherent upon her sex, which many women of the present day, even those to whom Mgr. Dupanloup dedicated his famous pamphlet, "Studious and learned women," would consider most severe. In this letter the austere tutor did not even mention the pagan authors which Rufinus accused him of

[1] Epist. cvii. ad Lætam, 1.   [2] *Ibid.*, 4.

continually quoting in his letters to women and young girls; but as Father Charles Daniel observed, "it was no longer a question of classical studies."[1] The only works which the child was to be allowed to study when she should be of an age to understand them, were sacred ones and the books of the authorised expounders of tradition. "Let her first study the Psalms and then model her life from the proverbs of Solomon. Let the books of Ecclesiastes teach her to despise the world, and let her seek lessons of patience and fortitude in Job. She should then pass on to the gospel which she should ever keep open before her, and her heart should be impregnated with the words of the Acts of the Apostles and the Epistles." Jerome then indicated the order in which Paula was to read the other portions of the scripture, as a prudent censor omitting the Apocrypha with its false titles and unorthodox doctrine, and as a careful theologian showing the young Christian maiden from which ecclesiastical authors she could draw the most irreproachable doctrine. The authors whom he mentioned were those whom unconsciously he emulated or rivalled. "She should always keep the treatises of Cyprian near at hand. She may safely peruse the letters of Athanasius and the books of Hilary. Give her full access to the works of these great geniuses, for her faith and her piety cannot be injured by such reading."[2]

The recluse was troubled by one misgiving: was it possible for Leta, who no doubt led a pious life,

[1] Classical Studies in Christian Circles, Chapter III.
[2] Epist. cvii. ad Lætam, 12.

yet lived in Rome amid worldly surroundings, to bring up her daughter according to such a system of education? The child should be removed from the perils of Rome. "Send her," he wrote, "to her grandmother and her aunt, place this rare pearl in Mary's cave in the manger where the infant Jesus lay. Nurture her in the convent amid choirs of virgins . that she may be ignorant of the world and live the life of an angel. Confide this child, whose very wails are prayers for thee, to Eustochium; confide Paula to her so that she may imitate and inherit her saintliness. Let her see, and love, and admire from her earliest childhood the woman whose speech, deportment and bearing are lessons in virtue. Let her be rocked in the arms of her grandmother, who will do for her all that she did for her own child, and who, through long experience, has learnt the art of bringing up, instructing and guarding virgins." The instincts of paternal love and solicitude latent in the soul of the aged saint seemed to have been awakened; he asked to be allowed some share, no matter how humble, in the child's education. "If you send me Paula," he said, "I promise to become her tutor and her nurse. I will carry her upon my shoulders, and, old man that I am, hold lisping intercourse with her, prouder of my occupation than ever Aristotle was of his. For I shall be forming the character, not of a King of Macedonia destined to perish by poison at Babylon, but of a handmaid and a bride of Christ, an inheritor of the Kingdom of Heaven." [1]

Jerome's wish was not immediately granted. There

[1] Epist. cvii. 13.

came a day, however, when the youthful Paula joined her aunt, whom she survived, at the Convent of Bethlehem, where she too was submitted to the abominable persecutions of the Pelagians. After the death of Eustochium, Jerome commended Paula to Alypius and to Augustine in a letter written in 419, possibly the last he ever wrote.[1]

Long before this, in 404, the elder Paula, of glorious memory, had entered upon her heavenly reward. The end, however, for which she yearned, had only been reached after terrible sorrows. She had been deeply afflicted by the death of her daughter Rufina, who from the Ostian shores had tearfully entreated her to defer her departure at least until after her marriage.[2] Although the intrepid Christian had had the courage to place seas and deserts between herself and those she loved, yet she never knew either indifference or forget. Towards the end of 403 a fever forced Paula to take to her bed. Eustochium watched at her side—an indefatigable nurse, who only left her mother while she slept, to visit our Saviour's manger. Jerome also stayed by the dying woman, experiencing a bitter joy at contemplating such a peaceful end, and in receiving her last utterances, which were still praises of her God. John, the Bishop of Jerusalem, the bishops of the neighbouring towns, and countless priests and deacons also assisted at Paula's death-bed, and celebrated magnificent obsequies for her in the cave of the Nativity.

[1] Epist. cxliii. ad Alypium et Augustinum.
[2] Ep. cviii. Epitaphium Paulae, 6.

Paula died upon the 26th of January 404, at the age of fifty-seven, having spent eighteen years of her life at Bethlehem. Jerome tells us that no sound of weeping was heard at her funeral, but that he, who began by restraining his grief, was overcome by it. "The death of the saintly and venerable Paula," he wrote Theophilus a few months later, "has so completely prostrated me that until to-day I have translated nothing from the holy books. Thou knowest how at one blow I lost my only comfort. ."[1] In the preface to his translation of the monastic rules of St Pachomius he makes a similar confession: The prostration of grief had long kept him silent, and if he had finally broken through this torpor and returned to his customary tasks, beginning with the translation of some works of the Abbots of Tabenne, it was in the hope that it would meet with the approval of the saintly soul who had always taken such a lively interest in monasteries.[2]

Eustochium begged Jerome to write her mother's funeral oration, and Jerome, who had already eulogised Blesilla, Paulina and Leah, and celebrated the priestly virtues of Nepotian, could hardly refuse her request. The more so that he had glorified Fabiola, the Christian descendant of the Fabii and formerly his guest in Palestine, in the most stirring accents. Fabiola, who had been one of the members of the pious gatherings on the Aventine, had died in 401, after expiating the weakness and ignorance which

---

[1] Epist. xcix. ad Theophilum, 2.
[2] Tillemont Memoires, etc. St Jerome, Art. cvi.

had permitted her to contract a second marriage during the lifetime of her unworthy husband, by the most heroic penances and by lavish charity. It was therefore incumbent upon the sincere and eloquent panegyrist of these saintly souls, to overcome his grief and extol the benefactress and peerless friend whose death seemed to have almost crushed him.

Even when he had overcome his hesitation, his first effort was fruitless. Who, indeed, when trying to narrate the life of one dear and departed, has not experienced the same anguish, has not felt conscious of his own impotence? The soul oppressed by grief is no longer master of itself; it has no command over its thoughts and memories; words fail it, or are at best but weak and halting. "Whenever I took up my stylus," wrote Jerome, "it slipped upon the wax of my tablets, my fingers became rigid, and the stylus fell from my hand; my brain seemed powerless."[1] Jerome finally decided to dictate, and in two vigils he composed the desired eulogy, which is a letter and a narrative but not a homily. We must not expect to find it a funeral oration such as Bossuet conceived, and of which he realised the sublime ideal, an oration centring all the events of a lifetime around one or two principal ideas, valuable examples of which have in modern times been given us by the Cardinal Pius. "Jerome," says Thierry, "followed Paula through all the phases of her life, her marriage, widowhood, consecration to the religious life, her domestic sorrows, and the persecution of

[1] Epist. cviii., 32.

those dear to her. He gives an account of her departure from Rome, their journey together in the Holy Land, their visit to the wilderness of Nitria, and their life at Bethlehem. It was the story of the twenty years they had passed in close proximity that he delighted to set before his absent friend. He omitted nothing, and in his narrative Paula seems alive once more; she speaks and walks, we hear the austere lessons which she addressed to her nuns, her controversies with heretical monks, even the gentle sallies of a mind incapable of bitterness. Her grief at the loss of her children, her wasting illness, and her last struggles with death, are all recorded and described with tearful emotion. Sacred memories of a friend, destined to awaken and to mingle with those of a daughter!"[1] If we do not make any extracts from the pathetic passages in which this funeral oration abounds, we must at least quote its peroration. " I call the Lord to witness," said Jerome, " that Paula has not only left her daughter completely destitute, but she has left her many debts, and what is even worse, a multitude of brothers and sisters, whom it is next to impossible to feed, and whom it would be wicked to turn away. Was there ever such an example of virtue ? A woman of the highest breeding, and formerly extremely wealthy, so impoverished by her own faith and charity that she almost reduced herself to starvation. . . Fear not, Eustochium, for the Lord is thine inheritance, and in this greatest inheritance of all, thy share is large. Now that thy

[1] St Jerome, Book x.

mother has been crowned by a long martyrdom thy cup of joy is full. It is not the shedding of blood which alone constitutes martyrdom; the faithful bondage of a soul wholly consecrated to God is a daily martyrdom, the crown for which is woven of lilies, while the crown of the bleeding martyr is woven of roses and violets. . . . To those who have conquered, be it in peace, be it in war, the same reward is given."

" Like Abraham of old, thy mother heard a voice, saying, 'Get thee out of thy country and from thy kindred and from thy father's house unto a land that I will show thee.' She heard the command which Jeremiah gave in the name of God, ' Flee out of the midst of Babylon and deliver every man his soul,' and faithful until the end, she never returned to Chaldea, never yearned for the tainted pleasures of Egypt, but accompanied by a choir of virgins, she went to inhabit the birthplace of her Lord, and from her lowly home in Bethlehem, raising her voice to heaven, she cried to God as did Ruth to Naomi, 'Thy people are my people, and thy God shall be my God.' . Farewell, oh Paula, may thy prayers support the declining years of him who reveres you. Thy faith and thy good works have gained thee access to Christ, once admitted to His presence thy prayers will be more surely heard."[1]

In the passage we have just quoted, Jerome made a slight allusion to the monks and the nuns which Paula's death had left so destitute. Providence,

[1] Epist. cviii. Epitaphium Paulae, 30, 31, 32.

however, continued to watch over the convents at Bethlehem. We already know how Jerome sold the last remnants of his patrimony in order to support his monks. And Eustochium, brave and generous as her mother had been, was soon joined by Paula, who, obedient to Jerome's bidding and to the supreme wish of her grandmother, brought ample funds to the nuns whose life she had come to share.

CHAPTER VII

CONTROVERSY WITH ST AUGUSTINE

THE controversy which a passage of St Paul's Epistle to the Galatians, differently interpreted by Jerome and Augustine, excited between the aged expounder of the Scriptures, who compared himself to Entellus in the Æneid, and the priest who had already become famous, and who later shed such unparalleled glory upon the hitherto obscure see of Hippo, took place between the years 395 and 405. A few historical details may help to explain the object of the controversy.

The Gospel had first been proclaimed to the Jews, just as the Messiah had first been promised to them. Their severe monotheism, the traditions and hopes which they held in trust, everything in the designs of God had prepared them to receive the new revelation, for, according to St Paul, the law of Moses was to be their guide to the Gospel. We know what resistance the unintelligent and intractable pride of many of the Jews opposed to the divine gift, and even among those who accepted Christianity there were many who, failing to understand its supremely new and liberating character, imposed the observance of the Mosaic rites upon the Gentiles as a necessary condition of their salvation. The question had been decided at the Council of Jerusalem, where, under the divine guidance, Peter the leader of the Twelve, and James the bishop of what were termed the Christians of the Circumcision, had agreed to emancipate the converted Pagans from the prescriptions of the law. All the Jewish Christians, however, did not allow themselves to be convinced. In the eyes of these staunch upholders of rites henceforward rendered useless, the only true Christians were those who conformed themselves to all the Mosaic observances, and who became in the Church what the "proselytes of the Temple" had been in the Synagogue; the others were the "proselytes of the Gate," with whom all the relations of life, all familiar intercourse were forbidden. At one moment, Peter had seemed to favour these unjustifiable claims. In the following fluent and dramatic language St Paul has given us an account of what has been called the "Conflict of Antioch." "But when Peter was come to Antioch, I withstood him to the face, because he was to be blamed. For before certain came from James, he did eat with the Gentiles: but when they were come, he withdrew and separated himself, fearing them which were of the circumcision. And the other Jews dissembled likewise with him; insomuch that Barnabas also was carried away with their dissimulation. But when I saw that they walked not uprightly according to the truth of the gospel, I said unto Peter before them all, If thou, being a Jew, livest after the manner of the Gentiles, and not as do the Jews, why compellest thou the Gentiles to live as do the Jews?"[1]

[1] Galatians ii., 11-14.

Let it first be clearly understood, that in whatever manner the passage which so agitated St Jerome and St Augustine may be interpreted, the doctrine of the infallibility of St Peter and the apostles, infallibility which, personal to these, has been perpetuated in the successors of St Peter—was not in question. The apostles' contention touched only upon a question of conduct.

Was this contention, however, real, or was it not rather a preconcerted scene between Paul and Peter who were both anxious to repress, by some startling example, the intolerable pretensions of the Judaisers? This was Jerome's opinion. " Paul," he wrote, " seeing the grace of the Gospel thus imperilled, as an experienced warrior had recourse to a new manœuvre; he wished to oppose another line of action to that by which Peter hoped to save the Jews, and to withstand the apostle of circumcision to his face. He did not really blame Peter's intention, and if he reproved him and publicly resisted him, it was in the interest of the Christians of Gentile extraction. Should it be maintained that Paul really resisted Peter, and that to uphold the truth of the Gospel he made his senior the object of a bold and public affront, it should no longer be said that Paul became a Jew in order to convert the Jews, and one would have to believe him guilty of deception when he shaved his hair at Cenchrea and made his offering at Jerusalem with a shorn head,[1] when he circumcised Timothy,[2] and when he walked barefooted, all of which were clearly a part of the Jewish cere-

[1] Acts xviii.   [2] Acts xvi.

monies. If Paul who had been sent to the Gentiles believed he had a right to say, 'Give no offence either to the Jews or to the church of God. .'; if, fearing to scandalise the Jews, he did certain things which were contrary to the liberty of the Gospel, by what right, or on what ground, dared he reprove Peter, the apostle of the Gentiles, for what he himself might be accused of having done? But as we have already said, Paul publicly opposed Peter and the others, that is, the Judaising party, so that the stratagem which, to the disadvantage of the Christians of Gentile extraction, imposed legal observances, might be corrected by a feigned rebuke. ."[2] In support of this theory Jerome alleged the authority of Origen, Didymus, Appollinaris, who was still a Catholic, Eusebius of Emesa, Theodorus of Heraclea,[3] and later that of John Chrysostom, whom the plots and violent measures of his friend Theophilus had lately caused to be deposed and banished.[4]

Augustine took exception to an interpretation which seemed to him to weaken the testimony of St Paul and the veracity of the Scriptures, and in a letter which the African priest Profuturus was intrusted to deliver to Jerome, he expressed himself upon the subject with half sorrowful severity ("dedit litteras familiares illas quidem, salibus tamen acrioris correctionis aspersas," said Baronius).

[1] 1 Cor. x. 32.
[2] Comment. in Epistolam ad Galatas. Lib. i, cap. 11.
[3] Comment. in Epistolam ad Galatas. Prologue.
[4] Epist. cxii. Hieronymi ad Augustinum, 6.

"I have read," Augustine wrote Jerome, "a commentary upon the Epistles of St Paul which is ascribed to you, and I came across the passage in the Epistle to the Galatians, where the Apostle Peter is reproved for the deception into which he had been drawn. I confess with no small sorrow that in it you, even you, or the author of this writing whosoever he may be, have defended the cause of untruth. I consider it a fatal error to believe it possible to find anything in the Scriptures which is untrue, in other words, to believe that the men to whom we are indebted for the sacred works could have inserted therein any falsehood. Once admit any officious untruth in the Holy books, then, in accordance to this pernicious principle, in order to escape from a moral which imposes too much restraint upon us, or from dogmas which are beyond our comprehension, we may attribute any part of these works to the artifice of an author who has not told the truth." Having pursued his urgent argument pointed by illustrations from the Bible, Augustine, scarcely hoping that his request would be acceded to, demanded an explanation which would dispel his doubts. In conclusion he claimed a fraternally severe criticism of which he had just given an example, for those of his works which Profuturus was to offer to Jerome.

Meanwhile Profuturus, who had been made Bishop of Cirta in Numidia, instead of starting for Palestine took possession of his see, where he very shortly died. The letter, therefore, which had been given to him never reached its destination, but unfortunately fell into indiscreet hands, and the copies of it which were circulated in Dalmatia and Italy, encouraged Jerome's enemies in their criticisms. Augustine had also been raised to the Episcopacy in 395, and amid new cares and duties had no doubt forgotten not only his letter, but the commentary which had provoked it, when a note which the deacon Presidius brought him from Jerome, recalled them to his mind. As Jerome's missive did not in any way answer the questions Augustine had put to him, the latter thinking that his letter had gone astray wrote another, which was longer but not less peremptory and no less aggressive. After having again tried to demonstrate the dangers of the hieronymian explanation, Augustine exhorted the aged historian to a courageous retraction of it, reminding him of the fable of Stesichorus who, struck with blindness by the demi-gods Castor and Pollux for having decried the chastity and beauty of Helen in a satire, did not recover his sight until he had sung the praises of the grace and virtue he had outraged, upon his lyre.

"I implore you," he wrote Jerome, "gird yourself with a sincere and Christian severity, correct and amend your work, and so to speak sing its recantation. The truth of Christians is incomparably more beautiful than the Helen of the Greeks, for it indeed, have our martyrs fought more bravely against the Sodoma of their century, than did the Greek heroes against Troy. I do not urge you to this disavowal, so that you may recover your mental sight, for God forbid that I should think that you had lost it, yet suffer me to tell you that through I know not what inadvertency you have turned aside your eyes, sound and far-sighted though they may be, and have failed to see the disastrous consequences of a system which would admit that one of the authors of our sacred books, could once, in some part of his work, have conscientiously and piously lied." [1]

The man, by name Paul, to whom this letter had been confided, overcome by his terror of the sea, did not embark for Palestine, and another messenger chosen by Augustine also failed to deliver the missive to Jerome. The letter, however, spread abroad, and with it a report that Augustine had composed and sent to Rome a book against Jerome. The deacon Sisinius, a friend of the hermit, found Augustine's letter, together with some other writings by the same doctor, on an island in the Adriatic, and lost no time in sending it to its destination.

This certainly was enough to rouse a soul less ardent, and a writer less harassed by envy, or less surrounded by admirers, quick to take alarm and even to be angered at all criticisms directed against their master; yet Jerome controlled himself and refrained from answering. He explained his silence in the letters which later he wrote to the Bishop of Hippo. It seems that, although he unmistakably recognised Augustine's familiar style and manner of argument, the material evidences of authenticity were wanting. Besides which, the veteran soldier of Orthodoxy shrank from opening hostilities with

[1] Epist. lxvii. Augustini ad Hieronymum, inter Epistolas Hieronymi, 7.

a bishop of his own communion whom he had loved before even knowing him, and who had sought him in friendship; one, who already illustrious, was to continue his scriptural works, and one in whom he gladly welcomed a legitimate heir.

When at last Augustine heard of the pain his letters, divulged in such an unaccountable manner, had caused in the solitude of Bethlehem, he wrote to Jerome: "A rumour has reached me which I have difficulty in believing, yet why should I not mention it to you? It has been reported to me that some brothers, I know not which, have given you to understand that I have written a book against you, and that I have sent it to Rome. Rest assured that this is false; God is witness that I have written no book against you" (the book in question was the letter, or letters, of which Jerome's enemies had taken a perfidious advantage). "If there be anything in my works contrary to your views, know or believe that it was written not to antagonise you, but to explain what seemed to me the truth. Point out to me anything in my writings which could offend you; I will receive your counsels as from one brother to another, glad to make any corrections, glad also of such a token of your affection. I ask and entreat this of you." Then followed one of those effusions in which Augustine's soul so often found its outlet. "Oh, why, if I may not live with you, may I not at least live in your vicinity, and hold sweet and frequent intercourse with you. But since that has not been granted me, consent at least to uphold and draw closer the ties which render us present to one another in the Lord: disdain not the letters which I will sometimes write you."[1]

Sincere and touching as were the tones of this letter, it failed to disarm Jerome, who did not think it sufficiently explicit. Moreover the advice, and even the appeals, which it contained offended the somewhat proud susceptibility of the aged biblical student. After evincing his doubts, which we have already mentioned, upon the authenticity of Augustine's letter, he proceeded to add these words: " God forbid that I should dare to censure the works of your Beatitude; let it suffice me to defend my own, without criticising those of others. Your wisdom knows full well that every man is wedded to his own opinion, and that it were childish boasting to imitate the youths of old who, by slandering famous men, sought to become famous themselves. Neither am I foolish enough to be offended by the divergences which exist between your explanation and mine. You yourself are not hurt at my holding different opinions. But where our friends have really the right to reprove us is when not perceiving our own wallet, as Persius says, we look at that of another."

" I have still one thing to ask of you, which is that you should love one who loves you, and that being young, you challenge not an aged man upon the battlefield of the Scriptures. We too have had our day, and we have run our race to the best of our abilities, and now that it has come to be your turn

[1] Ep. ci. Augustini ad Hieronymum, 2, 3.

to do likewise, and that you are making great strides, we have a right to rest. To follow your example in quoting the poets, remember Dares and Entellus, think also of the proverb which says, 'As the ox grows weary he plants his foot more firmly.' I dictate these lines with sadness; would to God I might embrace you, and that in brotherly intercourse we might have instructed one another. Think of me, saintly and venerable pontiff! See how much I love you, I who, although challenged, have been unwilling to reply, and who do not yet resign myself to ascribe to you what in another I should blame."

To this letter, which was brought him by the sub-deacon Asterius, Augustine made a modest and touching answer. He vindicated himself of having, so to speak, defied the aged athlete upon the field of the Scriptures, and merely asked to be enlightened. "Far be it from me that I should take offence, if by sound reasons you will and can prove to me that you understand the Epistle to the Galatians or any other like part of the Scriptures better than I. Far from resenting it, I should deem it a privilege to be instructed or corrected by you. But, beloved brother, you would not think that your answer could have hurt me, had you not thought that I had been the first to wound you. My best course is to acknowledge my fault, and to confess that I offended you in writing that letter which I cannot disown. If I offended you, I conjure you by the meekness of Jesus Christ do not render me evil for evil by offending me in your turn. Now, to dissimulate what you find to alter or correct in my writings or my discourses would be to offend me. . . . Reprove me with charity if you deem me in the wrong, innocent though I may be, or treat me with the tenderness of a father if you think me worthy of your affection. Innocent, I will receive your reproaches in a spirit of gratitude; guilty, I will acknowledge both your benevolence and my own error."

Jerome's allusion to the hardy Entellus furnished Augustine with the opportunity for the following humble confession: " What! shall I fear your letters, which are severe perhaps, but salutary like the gauntlets of Entellus? The aged athlete dealt Dares formidable blows, and felled him to the ground without curing him. But I shall receive your corrections with a quiet heart, for I shall not suffer through them, but be healed. You wish me to compare you to an ox; I consent, but to an ox who under the weight of years retains all his vigour, and in the divine acre pursues his fruitful toils. I prostrate myself before you. If I have done any wrong, trample upon me. The weight which has accrued to you with age is not too heavy, so long as my sin be crushed under your foot like a rush of straw."

Augustine then complained of the great distance which separated Hippo from Bethlehem, and of the endless delays to which their correspondence was subjected. How he would have liked to see and listen to the aged master! "I discover so much in those of your letters which have reached me, that my most earnest wish is to live at your side. I am thinking of sending one of my sons to your school should you deign to answer me, for I have not, and never shall have, your scriptural knowledge. What little I have I distribute among God's people, and my episcopal duties make it impossible for me to devote more time to such a study than is strictly necessary for the instruction of my people."[1]

Won by the humble and persuasive tones of this letter, Jerome answered it, and at last began the purely amicable controversy for which Augustine had asked. It has been said, however, that "before entering the lists he wished once for all to unburden his heart, so that the leaven of the past should in the future, no longer embitter their friendship or his own judgment. He gratified this desire in a letter of an entirely personal character, which acts as a sort of prologue to the second one which he wrote."[2] Jerome's explanations were at times frank to the point of harshness. An undercurrent of resentment runs through them, yet his anger was not unmixed with love.

He wrote, "Several of our brothers, pure vessels of Christ, such as may be found in great numbers in Jerusalem and the holy places, have suggested to me the thought that you did not act uprightly, but that enamoured of the vain clamour and glories of this world you sought to increase your reputation at the expense of ours, persuading the majority that when you challenge I tremble, and that you write as a scholar, but that I keep silence like an ignorant man, and that I have at last met someone who has

[1] Epist. cx. Augustini ad Hieronymum, 1, 2, 4, 5.
[2] Thierry, St Jerome, book xi.

known how to silence my loquacity. I frankly confess to your Beatitude that it was primarily for this reason I would not answer you. Besides which, I could not bring myself to believe that the letter was really from you, not deeming you capable of attacking me with as in the proverb, a sword immersed in honey. Moreover, I feared that I should be accused of arrogance towards a bishop, should I censure my censor, especially had I drawn attention to the passages in his letter which breathed of heresy. Finally, I should have given you good cause to complain of an inconsiderate answer, and to say to me, ' Did you verify my letter and recognise my signature before permitting yourself to thus outrage a friend and to brand him with the shame of the malice of others?' Also, as I have already written you, either send me the same writing signed by your hand, or else cease from challenging an aged man who is hidden in the depths of his cell. If you wish to display and show your learning, then seek out some of the noble and eloquent youths who I am told abound in Rome, who are able to combat you, and who would dare cross swords with a bishop. I, who was once a soldier, and am to-day a veteran, will sing your victories and the victories of others, but I cannot face a battle with a body which is exhausted by age. Still, should you persist in asking me for an answer, remember that the masterly inactivity of the aged Fabius Maximus defeated the youthful ouslaughts of Hannibal. ."

Jerome continued his recriminations and complaints, and concluded his letter with a paragraph in which are summed up the various sentiments which had inspired it. "Farewell, beloved, my son by reason of your age, my father by reason of your rank. I ask one thing of you: when you wish to write to me, pray do in such sort that I may be the first to receive your letters."[1]

In another letter[2] Jerome, drawing upon his resources of vehement powers of argument and vast erudition, defended the thesis which, following the example of illustrious predecessors, he had adopted. In certain parts of this letter, making an undue use of the *ex absurdis* argument, and imputing conclusions to his opponent which the latter would have had the right to disown, he reproached Augustine with resuscitating or abetting ancient errors. The Bishop of Hippo maintained that if Paul had sometimes practised the law, it was not that after the coming of the Messiah he thought it necessary to salvation, but to show that he did not disapprove of it, and that if he blamed the prince of the apostles, it was because his conduct exposed the Christians of Gentile extraction to the danger of considering legal ceremonies as obligatory. "Should this be true," exclaimed Jerome, "we fall into the heresy of Cerinthus and Ebion, who believed in Christ, and who have only been anathematised by the Fathers for having added legal ceremonies to his Gospel, who although professing the new doctrine, insisted upon retaining the ancient rites. And what of the Ebionites who call themselves Christians? To this very day they are perpetuated in all the synagogues in the East, a sect of

[1] Ep. cv. ad Augustinum, 2, 3, 5.
[2] Ep. cxii. ad Augustinum.

Mineans, known as Nazarenes, whom even the Pharisees condemn. They believe in the same Christ as we, the Son of God, born of the Virgin Mary, suffered under Pontius Pilate, who rose again from the dead; but wishing to be both Christians and Jews they succeed in being neither Jews nor Christians. If you thought it your duty to try to heal my slight wound which in reality is but the prick of a needle, I beg of you think of your own, which has every appearance of a lance thrust. Indeed the wrong of having given in the explanation of the Scriptures, various opinions of the ancients, is not so great as that of reintroducing a perverse heresy into the Church. If we are compelled to receive the Jews with their ceremonies, if we allow them to bring the rites of the synagogue into the Church, I say most sincerely that it will not be the Jews who will become Christians, but the Christians who will become Jews." With the same eloquence and spirit Jerome summed up the reasons which Augustine had alleged in support of his opinions, and he endeavoured to show that he and his adversary were more agreed than they believed. "Between your opinion and mine the difference is small. I maintain that Peter and Paul observed, or rather pretended to observe, the ceremonies of the law for fear of vexing the Jews who had become Christians. You say that their observance of them was no artificial dissimulation, but a charitable condescension; hat it was not a vain fear, but mercy, which drove them to pretend to be what they were not."[1] The lengthy answer of Jerome's adversary proves, how-

[1] Epist. cxii., 13, 17.

ever, that he and Augustine were less united upon this point than he would have us think. " Who is there," asked the bishop of Hippo, " in whose discourses and writings I can believe if it be true that Paul deceived his sons? The apostle said in the beginning, ' I call upon God to witness that I am not lying in what I write you,' and yet, through I know not what administrative dissimulation (nescio qua dispensatoria simulatione), he would have asserted that Peter and Barnabas were not acting uprightly according to the Gospel, and that he had resisted Peter to his face because he compelled the Gentiles to conform to Judaism." [1] Augustine passed over as completely unfounded, the resemblance signalised by Jerome between Peter's conduct at Antioch, when he drew aside from the Christians of Gentile extraction, and that of Paul, when by prudent economy, he practised himself certain Jewish rites. Paul's whole life and teaching attest that he did not wish the Christian salvation to be thought dependent upon these practices, but neither did he wish to be suspected of holding ceremonies which had been instituted by God, and which, in the divine scheme of things, prefigured the glorious realities of the future, profane or idolatrous.

Of the two theories St Augustine's was the one which prevailed, and even Jerome seems to have ended by yielding to it. At the time of his contention with the Pelagians, Jerome wrote the following decisive phrase: "Who can complain that he is denied what the Prince of the Apostles himself did

[1] Epist., cxvi. Augustini ad Hieronymum.

not have?"[1] Indeed, in the face of St Paul's distinct affirmation, no orthodox exegete of the present day would dare to represent the controversy of Antioch as the result of a preconcerted scheme between the two apostles, and as a sort of symbolical drama in which they were actors. Its true explanation is more simple. "Peter thought that he should spare the prejudices of the Jews amongst whom he was to exercise a great part of his administration, knowing that a command issued from Jerusalem was capable of raising impediments to his apostleship in the Jewish quarters of the whole world. Paul looked at things from a different standpoint. More especially the apostle of the Gentiles, he held that the Gentile Christians should be treated with the same consideration as others. He considered that the right, which after the Council of Jerusalem, the Gentiles had obtained to abstain from the circumcision and from the law of Moses, should certainly be as much respected as the right of the Jews to retain these practices. His love for the Church's liberty received a shock when he saw that Peter now seemed to disapprove of what he used formerly to practise in person. There were thus two different forms of apostolic zeal in opposition.[2] Peter had exceeded in his condescension to the Jewish Christians, but, although the leader of the apostles, he bravely and with meek humility received the warning which Paul gave him before the Church of Antioch.

[1] Dialog. 1 contra Pelagianos, 22.
[2] Lesêtre.—Holy Church at the time of the Apostles.

The controversy between Jerome and Augustine ended with assurances of cordial and respectful admiration, on the part of the young bishop. "I pray you," he wrote to his former antagonist, "spare me not your strictures when you think them salutary. No doubt according to ecclesiastical rank, priesthood stands subordinate to the Episcopate, but in many other things Augustine is subordinate to Jerome. Moreover, one should neither fear nor disdain to be corrected by an inferior in rank."[1]

The difference between Augustine and Jerome had also touched upon another point, which we will merely indicate. Augustine, fearing that Jerome's translations from the Hebrew might bewilder the Churches which knew only the Septuagint, had urged him rather to translate with the utmost care the Greek version, which was consecrated by long usage and unanimous respect, into Latin. Jerome, however, answered Augustine's somewhat tentative objections in the most decided manner. "Since I have corrected and translated the old version from Greek into Latin for the benefit of those who only understand our own language (Augustine does not seem to have known this), I do not pretend to abolish them. In my translation I merely wished to re-establish the passages suppressed or altered by the Jews, and elucidate the meaning of the original Hebrew, to the Latins. No one is forced to read it should they not wish to. Let them drink the old wine with contentment and, if they like, disdain our new."[2]

[1] Epist. cxvi. Augustini ad Hieronymum, 33.
[2] Epist. cxii. 20.

In spite of these dissensions, Augustine carefully and sympathetically followed the scriptural work of the aged master until his death. In "The City of God" he praised Jerome's commentary upon David, he more than once consulted the learned exegete, and finally applauded the supreme battle which the indomitable old man waged against the growing heresy of Pelagius.

The commentary upon the Epistle to the Galatians belongs to the scriptural studies which filled Jerome's life. In 406, he finished the explanation of the twelve minor prophets with a commentary upon the prophecy of Amos, and in a preface to the second book of this commentary he weighed the advantages and disadvantages attendant upon old age.

CHAPTER VIII

THE LAST YEARS OF ST JEROME'S LIFE—HIS LAST ORDEALS

IN their declining years, men look back sorrowfully upon their past and wonder what the brief and uncertain future, which is all they dare look forward to, has in store for them. Most of those who begin to feel oppressed by the burden of their years are incapable of restraining a sigh, which is sometimes bitter, sometimes manly or resigned, but which always attests to the hopeless impotence with which old age threatens or strikes the majority. Even Christians are not exempt from this feeling of regret. It was not a worldling, disillusioned without being weaned from mundane interests, not a slave of ambition whom the approach of old age filled with despair, but Joseph de Maistre, the most steadfast of believers, who, when over sixty, wrote these words, in which he somewhat exaggerated his weakness: "I am now but an aged prisoner, whose greatest privilege is to gaze out of the window." The saints, who set no value upon the things of this world, and in their isolation aspire only to the longed for end, gladly welcome the grim visitor who leads them towards it, and by lightening their burden, shortens their journey. "Old age," wrote Jerome, "is accompanied by many blessings and many evils. It frees us from the overbearing mastery of the senses, curbs our appetites, crushes our carnal impulses, increases wisdom, and whispers riper counsels. The evils imputed to it are the infirmities by which it is frequently attended. The eyes become dim, food loses its savour, the hand trembles, the teeth decay, the feet begin to totter, and are scarcely able to walk, the body seems fast losing its hold upon life, and many of its members are already a prey to death. And yet all things well considered, weighing evil against evil, it is worth suffering the infirmities of old age to be delivered from the aggression of sensuality, a mistress in herself more grievous and importunate than any other. Even old age, indeed, is not secure from her attacks; but it is one thing to be brought into contact with temptation, and another to succumb to it. Buried beneath dead ashes, the spark still seeks at times to rekindle, but it has no longer the power to cause a conflagration."[1]

Jerome's letters to Hedibia and Algasia, in which he solved the difficulties in certain passages of the New Testament, which these studious Christian women had propounded to him, were written almost at the same time as his commentary upon Amos, and are a continuation of his scriptural works.

The commentary upon David, written towards 407, drew upon its author censure of a different

[1] Comment. in Amos. Lib. ii.

order from that which had hitherto assailed him. In the explanation of a famous dream of Nebuchadnezzar, Jerome, turning his attention from the distant ages whose memories he was evoking to the calamitous time in which he was forced to live, recognised in the iron and the clay of the statue shown to the King of Babylon, a symbol and a prophecy of the various stages through which the Roman Empire was to pass. The iron, typified the ancient glory and the ancient power of the Romans; the clay, the humiliation of the times in which he wrote: "There was nothing more mighty or invincible than Rome at her outset; to-day there is nothing weaker: in our civil wars and in our wars with foreign nations, we are reduced to craving the aid of the barbarians."[1] A defiant spirit of patriotism was aroused by these confessions, and Jerome was obliged to justify himself. "If I have applied to the Roman Empire the words of Daniel upon the statue, which is shown to us in the Scriptures as at first powerful and now weak, lay not the blame upon me, but rather upon the prophet, for one should not flatter princes to the extent of undervaluing the truths of the Scriptures. Generalisation does no individual injury."[2]

Jerome dedicated the commentary upon *Isaiah*, from which this short defence has been extracted, and which had formerly been promised to St Paula, to Eustochium and Pammachius. While engaged upon this work he was taken ill, and upon his

[1] Comment. in Danielem. Lib i., chap. ii.
[2] Comment. in Isaiam. Lib. xi.

recovery he wrote to Eustochium these strong and serene words which Tillemont has so well rendered: " Knowing to whom I am indebted for every instant of my life, and knowing that my death was perhaps only deferred so that I might be able to accomplish the work upon the Prophets which I had begun, I devote myself exclusively to this task; and as from some lofty elevation I contemplate the storms and the shipwrecks of this world, which, however, I bemoan, and which cause me infinite distress. Completely detached from the things of the present, I think only of the future, and, paying no heed to the clamour and the judgments of men, my thoughts dwell exclusively upon the awful Judgment Day of God. And you, Eustochium, virgin of Christ, whose prayers guarded me during my illness, now that I am recovered, again implore for me the grace of Jesus Christ, so that, under the guidance of the same spirit which through the mouths of the prophets predicted the things to come, I may penetrate the clouds, pierce their obscurity, and hear the Word of God." [1]

It is possible that the tempests and storms mentioned by Jerome were the opposition by which he was incessantly harassed, but it is incontestable that they also were allusions to the evils to which the East was at that time a prey. At the end of the year 408 Alaric laid siege to Rome, which, in order to regain its liberty, expended immense sums; in 409 the King of the Goths again appeared before the walls of the Eternal City. During these years

[1] Comment. in Isaiam. Lib. xi.

of calamity Jerome kept reminding his correspondents of the duties of the Christian life, and recalling to them evangelical counsels, the practice of which seemed to be facilitated by so many disasters. In the midst of his exhortations to the widowed Agerucia to keep an inviolable continence from that time forward, and to pour abundant alms into the hands of the poor, he suddenly, at the thought of the universal ruin and the universal distress, exclaimed: "What! the vessel has foundered, yet I think of the cargo! If we, pitiable survivors, have hitherto been spared, it is due not to our own merits, but to the mercy of God. Innumerable and cruel nations have inundated Gaul. All which lies between the Ocean and the Rhine, and between the Alps and the Pyrenees, has been devastated by the Quadi, the Vandals, the Sarmatians, the Ulans, the Herulians, the Burgundians, and oh! unhappy republic! even by the Pannonians. Mainz, which was formerly an important town, has been taken and sacked, and thousands have been slaughtered in its church. After a long siege Worms has been destroyed, and Reims, a town of old so strong; Amiens, Arras, the Morinians who dwell at the extremities of the earth; Tournai, Spires, Strasburg, have passed under the rule of the Germans. With the exception of a few towns, Aquitania, Novempopulania, Lyonnais, and Narbonensis have been completely ravaged. Beyond the walls it is the sword which slays; inside them, hunger. I am unable to recall without tears the fate of Toulouse, which, until now, had owed its preservation to the merits of Exuperus, its saintly bishop. Even Spain trembles daily at the memory of the Cimbrian invasion, and her terror causes her to suffer continually, what others have suffered but once. Answer me, my daughter: Is this a proper moment for thee to think of remarrying? Who, I ask thee, wilt thou espouse? One who flies before the enemy, or one who resists him? Whatever thy choice, thou knowest what awaits thee!"[1]

Jerome also strove to inspire Julian, the Dalmatian, with the same feeling of scorn for a world which on every side was passing from its wretched people. He urged him, appealing to the man of wealth smitten through the loss of a great part of his fortune, and to the father and husband, smitten through the loss of his wife and daughters, whose death seemed to his faithful soul merely a temporary separation, to devote himself more than ever to the service of God and the poor, and to follow Pammachius and the saintly priest Paulinus in their path of complete renunciation. The date of a letter which Jerome wrote to the deacon Sabinianus may possibly be fixed at the same period. Sabinianus, after certain episodes in his dissolute career which had caused the death of several of his accomplices, and after a notorious scandal which exposed him to a formidable revenge, fled from Rome and concealed himself among the ranks of some Samnite brigands. He then succeeded in reaching Palestine, where he presented favourable letters from the deluded bishop who had ordained him, to Jerome, who intrusted him with the office

[1] Epist. cxxiii. ad Ageruchiam. De Monogamia, 16, 18.

of reader in one of the convents directed by Eustochium. The incorrigible seducer, however, pursued his evil ways even in the very cave of the Nativity. He persuaded a young girl, who had received the virgin's veil in Rome and who had renewed her vow in Jerusalem, to follow him, but at the very moment fixed upon for their flight all was discovered. The heads of religious communities were empowered to inflict severe punishment upon rebellious persons and fugitives. Sabinianus threw himself at Jerome's feet in mortal terror, and, weeping bitterly, promised to henceforward lead a life of repentance under the monastic rule. He obtained mercy, but his tears do not seem to have been very sincere, for once reassured as to the danger of severe chastisement, he fled from the convent where he was confined and resumed a vagabond and profligate life throughout the Syrian towns, hurling the vilest calumnies against Jerome and Eustochium. More affected by the well-nigh desperate peril of Sabinianus' soul than by his own injuries, the anchorite wrote him an eloquent letter, saying: " Have pity on thyself. Remember that God will some day judge thee. Remember the bishop from whom thou didst receive thy deaconship. Wonder not that the holy man should have been deceived when he ordained thee. God sorely repented of having anointed Saul, and among the twelve apostles even, there proved to be one traitor. Unhappy wretch, turn toward thy Saviour so that He may turn towards thee. Repent, so that God may repent of the awful judgment He has pronounced against thee.

Why, forgetful of thy own misdeeds, dost thou strive to traduce others? Why traduce a man who gives thee salutary advice? I assent to being a malefactor, which is the report of me which thou hast spread abroad. Then let us mingle our repentance. I assent to being a sinner, then let us together expiate our sins with our tears. Thinkest thou that my crimes may become virtues for thee? Thinkest thou that it will mitigate the evils of thy plight to have many companions in thy profligacy? At least shed a few tears upon the costly raiments which adorn thee in thine eyes, and know that thou art but a ragged and filthy mendicant. It is never too late to repent. Hadst thou lain wounded upon the road which leads from Jerusalem to Jericho, the good Samaritan would have put thee on thy horse again, and guided thee to the hostelry to be cared for. Wert thou lying in the tomb and already exhaling the odour of death, the Saviour would bring thee back to life. . ."[1]

While Jerome was writing these lofty and inspired letters to Sabinianus, Rome, which had stood so many sieges and which had long been in imminent peril, fell into the hands of the barbarians. Upon the 24th of August 410, Alaric entered by the Porta Salaria and delivered the Eternal City to pillage, fire, and the sword. Marcella, the illustrious and pious widow who had founded the first monastery in Rome, and who had encouraged Jerome in his biblical labours, was one of the victims of the catastrophe. Her abode upon the Aventine was in-

[1] Epist. cxlvii., ad Sabinianum lapsum, 4, 9.

vaded, but the intrepid Christian woman resolutely faced the Goths who resorted to torture in order to force her to surrender them treasures which she no longer possessed, having distributed them among the poor. "Marcella," wrote St Jerome, "seemed insensible to the torment of scourge and lash. She threw herself weeping at the feet of the barbarians, but her one prayer was that they would not separate Principia from her, and that the youthful virgin might be spared that, which because of her great age, she herself had no cause to fear. Jesus Christ softened the hardness of their hearts, and pity crept in among their blood-stained swords. After the barbarians had conducted Marcella and her companion to the basilica of St Paul the Apostle, there to find either a place of refuge or a sepulchre, Marcella burst into transports of praise. She gave thanks unto God for having preserved Principia's chastity, for having permitted that captivity should be powerless to impoverish her, for she had no need of daily bread being so filled with the spirit of God that she felt no hunger, and for being able to say in all sincerity, "naked came I out of my mother's womb and naked shall I return thither. The Lord gave and the Lord hath taken away. Blessed be the name of the Lord."[1]

A few days after these events Marcella expired. All these tragic tidings were brought to Palestine by some fugitives, and Jerome was simultaneously informed of the death of Marcella, of that of Pam-

[1] Epist. cxxvii. ad Principiam virginem, sive Marcellæ viduæ Epitaphium, 13.

machius for which no one seemed able to account, and of the fall of Rome. A few of the lamentations which the triumph of the Goths wrung from Jerome's patriotic soul, have already been quoted in the introductory chapter. The commentary upon Ezekiel was interrupted, and it was not until two years after the catastrophe that the hermit was at last able to write Marcella's funeral oration and "Epitaphium" for Principia. A letter intended to direct the education of the youthful Pacatula, written by Jerome to Gaudentius gives us some idea of the universal desolation and also of the inconceivable obstinacy of a world which defied every divine threat and punishment. "Oh, shame," he cried, "all is crumbling to dust and ashes, except our sins, which still flourish. Rome, the famous, the head of the universe has perished in the flames of a single conflagration, and there is no region whither exile has not driven its citizens. The churches, formerly so holy, have been reduced to ashes, but we are still given over to avarice. We live as if we had but one day to live, we build as if we were always to dwell here below."[1] Fugitives from Rome had landed upon every shore and had, figuratively speaking, inundated Palestine. "Who would have believed," asked Jerome in one of his prefaces to Ezekiel, "that Rome, whose victories had raised her above the universe, could have fallen and become for her people both a mother and a tomb? Who would have believed that the daughters of the mighty city would one day be wandering upon

[1] Ep. cxxxviii. ad Gaudentium de Pacatulæ infantulæ educatione, 4.

the shores of the East, of Egypt, and of Africa, servants and slaves. Who would have believed that Bethlehem would daily receive noble Romans, illustrious matrons reared in opulence, but now reduced to beggary! Powerless to succour them all, I grieve and weep with them, and, completely given up to the duties which charity imposes upon me, I have put aside my commentary upon Ezekiel and almost all study, for to-day one must translate the words of the scriptures into deeds, and instead of speaking saintly words one must act them."[1]

Jerome's refuge did not escape from the incursion of the barbarians. Towards the year 411 the Saracens invaded and ravaged the frontiers of Egypt, Palestine, Phœnicia, and Syria. Fresh exiles, notably Pinianus, his mother Albina, and his wife Melania, fleeing from the cruelties and extortions of the prefect Heraclius, who had revolted against the Emperor, came to the Holy Land from Africa. In the midst of endless trials, beset by duties and visits which scarcely left him any leisure, Jerome became more and more oppressed by the burden of his years. "In the hours of the night," wrote the indefatigable veteran, "hours which I earn or rather snatch, and which towards winter begin to be somewhat longer, by the light of a small lamp, I endeavour to dictate these lucubrations, such as they are, and absorbed in my exegetical labours gain some respite from the cares of a tormented soul. Besides the effort of dictating I find another difficulty, for my eyes, like those of the saintly patri-

[1] Comment. in Ezechielem. Lib. iii. præfat.

arch Isaac, have grown dim with age, and I cannot read by lamplight the Hebrew works which, on account of the exiguity of the characters, are almost unintelligible to me even in the daytime. As to the Greek commentaries, I can only read them through the eyes of my brothers."[1]

In spite of this, Jerome persisted in his work, and was about to enter upon a supreme struggle. In a famous letter to Demetrias, which was a sort of treatise upon virginity, he warned this young patrician maiden, who had sought refuge in Africa, against some errors, in which Tillemont professes to detect traces of Origenism. As of old, when with a resolute heart and a firm voice he had adhered to the teachings of the Pope Damasus, Jerome exhorted Demetrias to remain faithfully united to the Holy See. Having reminded the youthful virgin of the blows which Pope Damasus dealt to heresy, he wrote: " It is my religious affection which prompts me to warn thee; keep the faith of Innocent, the son and successor of Anastasius upon the Apostolic throne, and however wise and well informed thou mayest think thyself, never embrace a strange doctrine."[2]

In 415 the Spaniard, Paulus Orosius, a disciple of Augustine, arrived in Bethlehem bearing letters in which the bishop of Hippo propounded two questions to the aged doctor. He consulted him upon the meaning of St James' text, " For whosoever shall keep the whole law and yet offend in one point

---

[1] Comment. in Ezechielem. Lib. xii., cap. xxi.
[2] Epist. cxxx. ad Demetriadem. De servanda virginitate.

he is guilty of all,"[1] and closed his letter with the following humble words: "Should thy erudition find anything to censure, I implore thee to write and tell me of it, and do not fear to correct me. One would indeed be unfortunate could one not listen respectfully to a man who has worked so much and with so much edification, and could one not give thanks to the Lord our God, who made thee what thou art, for the success of thy work. If it is my duty to be more disposed to learn from whomsoever it may be, that which it is well for me to know, than to impart my knowledge to others, how much more natural it is, that I should be ready to accept this service of charity from one whose erudition has, in the name and with the help of the Lord, advanced the study of the Scriptures to an extent hitherto unheard of."[2]

In another letter the bishop questioned Jerome upon the origin of the soul. This was not the first time that this question had been submitted to Jerome, for as early as 411 the Governor of Africa and his wife Anapsychia had laid it before him. The problem was, whether the human soul was immediately created by God at the very instant when nature ordains it to be united to the body, or whether the theory of a spiritual generation, causing one soul to proceed from another, were admissible. Upon this point Augustine had hesitated, and, as Cardinal Norris says, the audacity of the Pelagian party in

---

[1] James ii. 10.

[2] Epist. cxxxii. Augustini ad Hieronymum seu liber de sententia Jacobi, 21.

declaring original sin to be irreconcilable with the "creationist" doctrine, inclined the bishop of Hippo towards the contrary opinion.[1] St Augustine tells us, that in his answer, Jerome pleaded his absence of leisure to solve the problem; and as a matter of fact he did not solve it in any subsequent letter.[2] Although vehemently disclaiming the Origenist error of the pre-existence of souls, he does not seem to have adopted any solution of the difficulty, either in his books against Rufinus, or in his letters to Marcellinus. Jerome was not the only learned doctor with whom the question has remained undecided. In the twelfth century St Anselm prayed upon his death-bed that God might grant him a few days more of life in which to elucidate it, not that he was, as Charles de Rémusat tells us, one of those "great restless souls who prefer love to possession, and upon the threshold of heaven sigh for the labour and the hope of their earthly existences," but because as a religious thinker he would have wished to bequeath to his brethren one truth the more. The slow and sure workings of Catholic theology, under the direction and with the authority of the priesthood, have definitely solved the problem which tormented Augustine and Anselm, and raised the primarily contested theory of the immediate creation of souls, to the rank of other positive doctrines.

"Orosius," wrote Tillemont, "left St Augustine occupied in combating the Pelagians; he found St

---

[1] Vindiciæ Augustinianæ, cap. iv. 3.
[2] Retractat, lib. xii., cap. xlv.

Jerome engaged in the same war."[1] It was in this war that Jerome expended all his remaining strength.

The great Eastern heresies had touched upon the mysteries of the divine life, and had ended in offering their supporters a false explanation of them. Pelagius, an Irishman and a shrewd and daring spirit, fixed the general attention upon human nature, and professed to elucidate the mystery of the relations existing between created liberty and the concurrence and grace of God. There were two terms, one of which Pelagius suppressed, only acknowledging that of free will. According to him, a man possessing the divine gift of liberty could perform every duty, even the most difficult, avoid all sin, and become invulnerable to the impulses of passion. The innovator also rejected the dogma of original sin. Nature was good and sufficient unto itself; it needed no healing remedy, nor any assistance which would raise it to higher spheres. The idea of the Redemption, "that great remedy granted to a great distress,"[2] was dying out, and even prayer was arrested as if stifled upon human lips, from whence it nevertheless springs spontaneously. "If the grace of God consist in that He has given us the use of our own will," wrote Jerome, drawing legitimate conclusions from the theories advanced by Pelagius, "if satisfied with our liberty we consider that we had no longer need of His help, fearing that this very dependence might destroy our freedom of will, we should no longer pray nor try, in order daily to

[1] Memoirs, etc., St Jerome. Art. cxxxv.   [2] Gerbet.

obtain a gift which once received remains for ever in our power, to move the divine mercy by our supplications. . Let us also abolish fasting and continence; why should I exert myself to obtain through labour that which already belongs to me?"[1] All the rationalism of future ages was anticipated in this haughty system which undervalued human weakness and rejected all divine assistance. One can already hear the arrogant sophism of Rousseau: "I converse with God; I bless him for his gifts, but I do not pray to Him. What should I ask of Him?"

Pelagius had in turn taken his false doctrine to Italy, Africa and Palestine. In Rome he had won the protection of Melania, the illustrious widow. During a brief space of time the bishop of Hippo had also yielded to his charm, and Jerome had sympathetically received the innovator who knew how to regulate his speech and his silences according to circumstances. There were two disciples who propagated the doctrines of Pelagius with indefatigable zeal, one Celestius, who was less prudent or more daring than his master, and Julianus of Eclana, a former pupil of St Augustine and a friend of St Paulinus of Nola, who sang his Epithalamium in the most poetic language. Jerome soon discovered the true sense and import of the assertions of Pelagius, and urged thereto by the faithful who referred to the defender and tried interpreter of the true doctrine, he finally determined to write to Ctesiphon his letter against the new heresy.

"Perhaps none of his books," said Amédée Thierry,

[1] Epist. cxxxiii. ad Ctesiphontem, 5.

"better reveals the marvellous acuteness of St Jerome's mind. To pass judgment upon such a man as Pelagius, he had but the vague data which he had been able to collect from public rumour, from the reports of a few friends, or from the adroitly calculated conversation of the monk himself; of the audacious preachings of Celestius, or of the Pelagian writings which were beginning to spread over the East, Jerome knew practically nothing. ... A few of the Pelagian propositions, shrouded in circumlocution and mystery, were sufficient to enable him to reconstruct the whole of Pelagianism, to point out its dangers to the Faith, and to furnish weapons against its leader."[1] The letter to Ctesiphon, from which we have lately made quotations, contains a testimony which, without pride, but in tones of legitimate assurance, Jerome the septuagenarian rendered to the immaculate orthodoxy of his long life exclusively spent in the quest of truth. "From my youth ... since when, many years have elapsed ..." he said, "until my present age, I have written many works. I have ever been solicitous to set nought before my readers but that which I had learnt from the public teachings of the Church, and to follow, not the arguments of the philosophers, but the simplicity of the apostles; for I remembered this verse, 'For it is written, I will destroy the wisdom of the wise, and will bring to nothing the understanding of the prudent,' and again, 'Because the foolishness of God is wiser than men and the weakness of God is stronger than men.'[2] I defy

[1] St Jerome, Book xii.   [2] 1 Cor. i. 19, 25.

my adversaries; let them examine every book which I have written up till this moment, and if they find that I have made any mistake from lack of competence let them publicly denounce it, or else let them correct those things which are right and I will refute their calumnies; or should there be any foundation for their criticism, I will acknowledge my error, for I would rather correct myself than persevere in erroneous ideas."

Beside this letter to Ctesiphon, famous in the history of the Pelagian controversy, Jerome wrote his three "Dialogues," in which he quoted the Pharisaical prayer of the heresiarch, "Lord, Thou knowest that my hands are clean of plunder and my lips pure of lies; it is with these lips that I implore Thy mercy."[1] Words which may or may not be Pelagius' own, but in which breathe the whole Pelagian spirit of pride. In opposition to this vainglorious formula Jerome cited the humble petitions contained in the Lord's prayer. " Forgive us our trespasses. . lead us not into temptation but deliver us from evil." He invoked the testimony of the liturgy which Bossuet surnamed the "chief instrument of tradition."[2] " If you acknowledge but one baptism, the same for infants and adults, it is clear that infants receive it for the sins they have contracted in Adam."[3] Jerome did not omit the testimony of the divines; after alleging that of St Cyprian, he confronted his contradictor with

---

[1] Dial. adversus Pelagianos. Lib. iii. 14.
[2] Instruction sur les états d'oraison. Traité i., livre vi. n. 1.
[3] Dial., Lib. iii. 19.

the authority, at that time so weighty, of the bishop of Hippo. "Since long ago the pontiff Augustine wrote against thy false doctrine concerning the baptism of infants, two books which he dedicated to the tribune Marcellinus, the innocent victim of the tyrant Heraclius and of the heretics ... he wrote a third denouncing those who say as thou dost, that if man be willing, he may preserve himself from sin without the help of grace, and has lately written a fourth for Hilarion refuting thy false system. It is said that he is writing other books especially directed against thee, but they have not reached me. Not wishing to be reminded of Horace's lines, 'Do not carry timber to the forest,' I am inclined to cease this work. I should but uselessly reiterate the same things, or if I wished to say new ones, that brilliant genius has already said them better than I."

Jerome did not desert the battlefield. To escape from it he would have been obliged to leave Palestine, which was then ringing with the Pelagian controversy. The general disquiet which was thus agitating the Church no doubt decided bishop John to open, in July 415, the Conference of Jerusalem, which was entirely composed of priests, from among whom a few Europeans—Avitus, Vitalis and Passerius—equally versed in Latin and in Greek, were to serve as interpreters. Domninus, an orthodox and wealthy layman, formerly the controller of the imperial largess and invested by the Emperor Arcadius with the title of vicar of the prefects, sat also in the assembly.

In the absence of Jerome, who perhaps had not been bidden to the conference, Orosius attended in all the ardour of his youth and intrepid faith. He reported the condemnation passed upon Celestius by the Council of Carthage, and was loud in his praise of Augustine's and Jerome's refutations of the new dogmas. Pelagius when called upon to explain himself, did so in an ambiguous manner; the only daring which he evinced was in the contempt which, to the indignant stupefaction of the assemblage, he showed for the bishop of Hippo. The arch heretic knew himself to be protected by the benevolent attitude of John, whose misadventures in the Origenist matter had failed either to warn or make him amend his ways.

The conference dispersed after having decided that letters and deputies should be sent to Pope Innocent, and after having enjoined silence upon all. This silence, however, was broken by the bishop of Jerusalem, who accused Orosius of having advanced a heresy diametrically opposed to that of Pelagius. Orosius wrote his Apology and the controversy was reopened. Moreover, two Gallic bishops, Heros of Arles and Lazarus of Aix, driven from their province by political difficulties and drawn to Palestine by their desire to make a pilgrimage, denounced at that very moment the heresies of Celestius and Pelagius to Eulogius, the metropolitan of Cæsarea. A council was convened at Diospolis, the Greek name of the ancient city of Lydda, at which Heros and Lazarus, one of whom was ill, did not appear. Orosius, possibly prevented by secret intrigues from attending, was also absent. However, the memorandum upon which Heros and Lazarus had recorded a certain number of erroneous propositions was read at the Council, and Pelagius was called upon either to justify himself or to retract. With the aid of evasions, sophistical distinctions, or audacious denials, Pelagius succeeded in convincing of his innocence the fourteen bishops presided over by Eulogius and assembled at Diospolis. He was absolved, but Pelagianism was condemned; from whence the diverse opinions of a conference whose verdict " Pope Innocent would neither censure nor approve," have arisen. The bishop of Hippo has laid the responsibility of this verdict upon Julianus of Eclana. St Jerome, on the contrary, has found no better epithet to describe the Council of Diospolis than that of "contemptible."[1] Pelagius had disavowed his errors merely with his lips, in his heart neither he nor any of his party had the slightest intention of laying down their arms. His heresy was gaining ground in Europe and even in the East; in Asia, which until then had only been engrossed in metaphysical questions, Pelagianism excited considerable sympathy. Theodorus, the bishop of Mopsuestia, in Cilicia, and the apostle of the heresy which, disowning Christ's one and divine personality, attributed a separate personality to our Lord's humanity, favoured the false doctrines of Pelagius, and even wrote a book against Jerome which he later had the courage to destroy. Can one wonder at the secret affinity which drew to-

[1] Tillemont, St Augustine. Art. cclx.

gether the adversaries of grace and the future apostles of a heresy which was to debase Jesus Christ to the rank of a human being ? As I have already said elsewhere, " if Christ be not God, grace, which is the fruit of his blood and sufferings, must lose its inestimable dignity and its priceless worth. If that were the case, why consider grace to be the succour without which the human will, although capable through its own strength of acts morally good, can never accomplish deeds worthy of heaven ? The practical naturalism of the Western heretics and the speculative rationalism of those of the East sought one another across the distance which divided them, that they might embrace." [1]

The discussion of ideas and text did not satisfy the bellicose ardour of the Pelagians. Even the calumnies directed against Jerome did not satiate their relentless animosity. The coarse and ignorant rabble which too often forms the rearguard of factions, soon added material violence to these less tangible offences. One night in the year 416 the convent at Bethlehem was broken into, and St Augustine tells us that "a band of lost souls who, it is said, serve the perverse designs of Pelagius, gave themselves up to the most incredible outrages. The servitors of God, both male and female, who dwelt in this refuge under the guardianship of Jerome were cruelly beaten. A deacon was killed. The buildings of the monastery were set on fire, and Jerome only escaped from this furious assault

[1] History of ecclesiastical history. St Cyril of Alexandria and the Council of Ephesus.

by taking refuge in a tower"[1]—the same tower which later afforded refuge to the monks against the Arab invasions, and wherein Eustochium and her niece, Paula, fugitive and half-naked but always intrepid, also succeeded in concealing themselves.

The bishop of Jerusalem had foreseen nothing and had arrested nothing; he took no steps toward restoring the ruins or towards consoling the victims. Vanity and obstinacy had rendered this venerable person, who at that time was completing his thirtieth year of episcopacy, a more or less conscious accomplice of revolting deeds of violence. It was of course possible to ask the governor of Cæsarea for material protection, but Jerome, Eustochium, and Paula, feeling the necessity of seeking a higher authority as well, addressed themselves to the Pope, St Innocent. Aurelius, the metropolitan of Carthage, transmitted their grievances to the Pontiff, but the merciful discretion of the supplicants omitted the names of the guilty, and the Pope in his answer to Jerome was able to say, "Moved by the spectacle of such great misfortune we are prepared to exert the authority of the Apostolic See to punish the crime, but thy letter does not designate to us the criminal upon whom we are to visit our displeasure, and does not formulate any precise accusation." [2]

The Pope severely reprimanded the bishop of Jerusalem. "What preventive measures didst thou take? And when the calamity took place what consolation, what assistance didst thou proffer the

[1] De gestis Pelagii, 66.   [2] Epist. cxxxvi.

victims, who say that they fear still worse evils than those which they have already suffered?"[1]

John had died by the time Innocent's letter reached Jerusalem in 417, and under his successor Jerome was able to breathe more freely, for although some of the Pelagians continued to live in Palestine, at least their leader had been banished from it. "Know," Jerome wrote to the Aquilanian priest Riparius, in language which continually reminds us of Sallust " that Catiline has been driven from Jerusalem and from the whole province, not by any human power, but by the command of Jesus Christ himself. But I grieve to say that many of his conspirators still remain with Lentulus at Joppa.'[2] In apprising another friend, Apronius, of the distress to which he had been reduced, and of the peace which he at last enjoyed, Jerome wrote: " Your best course would be to leave all and come to the East, especially the Holy Land, for here all is tranquil. Doubtless the hearts of the heretics are still filled with venom, but they dare not open their impious mouths, and are like asps who stop their ears so as to hear nothing. Our house, as far as temporal goods are concerned, has been shaken to its very foundation by the violence of the heretics, but thanks to Christ it abounds in spiritual blessings, and it is better to have nought but bread to eat than to lose one's Faith.'"[3]

No mention has yet been made of Jerome's last scriptural work, his commentary upon Jeremiah,

---

[1] Epist. cxxxvii.   [2] Epist. cxxxvii. ad Riparium.
[3] Epist. cxxxix. ad Apronium.

which was frequently interrupted by the Pelagian persecution, and of which he only finished thirty-three chapters. He was growing weak and fast losing his hold upon life. He could scarcely speak, and was obliged to lift himself upon his wretched pallet by the aid of a rope when he wished to give instructions to his monks.

A supreme trial was reserved for the evening of Jerome's life. In the course of the year 418, Eustochium, at the age of fifty, thirty-four years of which had been spent in the convent of Bethlehem, fell asleep in the Lord. As Jerome wrote to his friends in Africa, Alypius and Augustine, such a sorrow caused him to disdain the outrageous writings of Anianus, the Pelagian. Providence, however, had not left him alone in his affliction, for the youthful Paula, whom he loved as if she had been his grandchild, was by his side. "This," said Thierry, "was the third generation of women which the most illustrious of the great Roman houses had sent to the Dalmatian priest to be to him a guardian angel in the desert; this last was the angel who ministered to him upon his death-bed."[1] A handful of people which the course of events had led from Rome to Hippo and from Hippo into Palestine, namely, Pinianus, his mother Albina, and his wife Melania, the heiress of a famous name, also surrounded the aged Saint with pious cares. Jerome passed away, close to the cave of the Nativity, on the 30th of September 420, leaving, we are told, the direction of his

[1] St Jerome, Book xii.

monastery to Eusebius of Cremona, and bequeathing to the entire Church immortal examples and immortal works.

There is no saint who lends himself less easily to legend than does Jerome, for his whole life is known to us; his works and his letters enable us to follow him through most of it; yet legend has fastened upon him. Should this cause astonishment or dissatisfaction? Legend was an homage which memory and popular imagination rendered to a man whose moral stature surpassed all ordinary proportions. Of the facts which legend has embroidered upon the austere woof of a simple and laborious existence I will mention but one—the incident of the wounded lion whom Jerome healed, and who became the guardian of the monks of Bethlehem and assisted them in their rustic labours. This lion, who must be closely related to the wolf tamed by St Francis of Assisi, has escorted, if I may so express it, the hermit throughout many centuries, has served him as a symbol, and appears stretched at the feet of the dying Saint in Domenichino's picture.

But, after all, like many other symbols, it has a foundation of truth; the generations of artists who have depicted the bishop of Hippo clasping in his hand the heart which, when finally weaned from unworthy affections, steadfastly adored the truth, were as justified in so doing as in giving Jerome the lion as symbol. None of the Fathers of the Church has better exemplified the characteristics of this noble animal such as they are described to us in natural history, in fables or in poetry. Jerome was intrepid and generous; he faced his adversaries without pausing to count their number or to measure their strength; and if at times a mighty roaring escaped him, it was the cry of a soul devoted to and desirous of truth alone; and if he were subject to violent outbreaks of wrath, his anger was often the anger of love.

THE WORKS AND THE TEACHINGS OF ST JEROME

CHAPTER I

THE WORKS OF ST JEROME

OUR readers are by this time familiar with the works and the teachings of St Jerome, for it would be well-nigh impossible to write the life of this great man without making frequent quotations from the pages in which he has given us a most life-like and sincere portrait of himself, and the narrative of his life would indeed be incomplete were the doctrines and doctrinal controversies which so largely filled it, passed over in silence.

Jerome was before all, and therein lies his principal claim to fame, the commentator and translator of religious literature. It has already been mentioned, and it will be sufficient to recall the fact, that the whole of the New Testament and all the protocanonical books of the Old Testament, that is to say those which belonged to the Jewish Canon, and of which the sacred character had never been questioned, underwent revision or translation at his learned hands. Of the deuterocanonical portions of the Old Testament, the portions which were the object of suspicions shared by Jerome but definitely removed at the Council of Trent, he only translated the books of Tobias and Judith, and the disputed passages of Daniel and Esther.

Jerome's reverend love for Holy Writ did not recognise individual fancy or private judgment as having any right to interpret it: he considered that the authority which guarded it should also expound it. "When Philip asked the man of Ethiopia, the Eunuch of great authority under Queen Candace who was reading the works of the prophet Isaiah: Understandest thou what thou readest? he answered, how can I except some man should guide me? As for me, if I may be allowed to speak of myself, I say that I am no more of a saint or no more zealous than this stranger who, leaving his Sovereign's court, had journeyed to the Temple from the remotest part of Ethiopia; who loved the divine laws and teachings to the point of reading the Scriptures in his chariot; but who, although absorbed in meditating and repeating the oracles of the Lord, still ignored Him whom, without recognising, he worshipped in the Holy Bible. Philip came and revealed to him Jesus concealed in the Scriptures as if under the rind of a tree. The Ethiopian was instantly convinced, he was baptised, became a believer and a saint, and from having been a disciple became a doctor. He learned more from the solitary spring into which the Church immersed him, than he had learned under the gilded canopies of the synagogue."[1]

[1] Epist. liii. ad Paulinum, 5.

In a letter to Pammachius, Jerome, the translator of the Holy Scriptures, expressed his ideas upon the proper manner of translating. He frankly confessed, justifying himself by the example of Cicero and Terence and by Horace's precepts, that when translating Greek works into Latin, he did not bind himself to be scrupulously literal; his desire was faithfully to render the authors' thoughts, and, when he considered it necessary, adapt the forms and figures of speech which they employed to the character of his own language. From this rule, however, which Jerome had established for his own use, he excepted the translation of the Scriptures in which he said "there is some mystery even in the very order of the words" (Ubi et verborum ordo mysterium est)[1].

Of the language and the style employed in the hieronymian version of the Bible, Villemain said—and we cannot do better than to repeat his able and just words upon the subject, that "human language has never received a more violent shock than in this sudden outbreak of the thoughts of the prophets and biblical hyperbole into the idiom of Cicero. The result is indeed unique, partly owing to the literal translation which introduces such strange forms into the Roman tongue, and partly because of the coined words with which the learned hermit of Bethlehem was inspired by his zeal and by his efforts to emulate the text."

In the course of this biographical sketch, mention has been made of Jerome's biblical commentaries which, with the exception of the later ones, he has

[1] Epist. lvii. ad Pammachium.

himself enumerated in the last chapter of his "De Viris Illustribus."

"It may truly be said," wrote Richard Simon, a critic against whose true worth we must not allow ourselves to be prejudiced by his irreverence, and his, at times, excessive audacity, "that in his knowledge of Hebrew, Chaldean, Greek and Latin, Jerome possessed the necessary qualities for properly interpreting the Scriptures in a greater degree than all the other Fathers. Not only had he read and examined the Greek versions in Origen's 'Hexapla,' but he had also frequently conferred with the most erudite Jews of his day, and he rarely took any steps in his scriptural work without first consulting them. In addition to this he had read every author, both Greek and Latin, who had written upon the Bible before him, and finally, he was well versed in profane literature. .

"Jerome's best method was the one which he employed in compiling his Commentaries upon the books of the Prophets, in which he first gave the ancient Latin version then in usage, adding to it a new one which he had made from the Hebrew text; he then compared the ancient Greek versions in his Commentaries so as to better understand the value of the Hebrew words. . . . Indeed we have no author from whom we may better gather the literal meaning than from Jerome. . . . No author who can instruct us more thoroughly in the criticism of the holy books than do the works of this Father. . ."[1]

Jerome did not only expound the Bible in the biblical commentaries which he has left us, but

[1] Critical History of the Old Testament, Book iii. chap. 9.

many of his letters are of an exegetical character. In letters written to the Pope Damasus, to Evangelus and Dardanus, and to many monks and women who without personally knowing him turned towards him from the different standpoints of Christianity, craving his instructions, Jerome strove to solve the difficulties submitted to him, and to conciliate the diversities and the apparent contradictions in the sacred story.

Jerome was skilled in polemic as well as in exegesis and criticism. His treatises against Helvidius, Jovinianus and Vigilantius, his dialogue against the disciples of Lucifer of Cagliari, his answers to John of Jerusalem, and his dialogue against the Pelagians, are all examples of his polemical writings.

In these hostile works, which contain passages of great eloquence, but which are by no means free from faults, Jerome's fiery spirit had full play.

Jerome's great strength lay in the fact that he maintained against his adversaries the position of a steadfast champion of tradition, a field which he knew well, and upon which, like Bossuet in later years, he was thoroughly in his element.

With what precision and with what a masterly touch did the bishop of Meaux quote, summarise, and judge his illustrious predecessors, the Fathers whose imposing tradition he has continued. Jerome also, had studied his predecessors, and knew how to characterise them. He enumerated them in a letter to Magnus, the orator, beginning with the Greeks. Quadratus, a disciple of the Apostles, and bishop of Athens, who had offered an apology of the Christian religion to the Emperor Hadrian, and whose alert and inquisitive mind had led him to Eleusis; the eloquent Aristides, another who had defended Christianity before the same prince of justice; Meliton of Sardis; Apollinaris of Hierapolis; Denis of Corinth, and Irenæus of Lyons, the historian of the early heresies. Jerome also mentioned Origen; the Roman senator Apollonius, whose eloquent apology has been found in the present century; Julius Africanus; Gregory Thaumaturgus; Denis of Alexandria; Anatole of Laodicea; the priest Pamphilus, Pierus, Lucian, Malchion, Eusebius of Emesa; Triphilus of Cyprus; Asterius of Scythopolis; the venerable confessor Serapion and the illustrious Cappadocians, Gregory, Basil and Amphilochus.[1]

Then follow the Latins: "Tertullian, whose Apologetica and whose works against the nations are a reservoir of secular knowledge; Minucius Felix, a Roman lawyer, who in his 'Octavius' and in his book against the astrologers (providing the title of this last work is correct) has touched upon all the works of pagan literature, 'either to make use of or to refute.'" "The blessed Cyprian resembles a pure spring from which well sweet and tranquil waters." The language of Victorinus, who received the martyr's crown, did not do justice to his thoughts. Lactantius recalls to me the flood of Ciceronian eloquence. Would to God he had established our beliefs as effectually as he destroyed the adverse heresies. Arnobus is unequal and exaggerated; a faulty arrangement

[1] Epist. lxx. ad Magnum Oratorem Urbis Romae, 4.

renders his work confused. St Hilarion speaks in obsolete heroics; the flowers of Greek rhetoric with which he adorns his style, the long periods in which he envelopes it, renders it almost unintelligible to the unlearned reader. [1]

In the reign of the Emperor Constans the priest Juvencus wrote the history of our Lord in verse, and did not shrink from subjecting the majesty of the Gospel to the laws of metre.[2]

Jerome waged his war against the innovators, attended by all these witnesses, and armed with the resources they afforded him. He confronted their audacious denials not only with positive texts, but with the constant usage of the Church. Thus, to Vigilantius, a scoffer at the cult of relics, he showed the Roman Pontiff and all the bishops of the world, offering the eucharistic sacrament upon the tomb of the martyrs. He had, ere this, pleaded the teachings and the traditional uses of the Church to the partisans of Lucifer of Cagliari who, in their fierce zeal, declared the bishops who had signed the inadequate formula of Rimini to have irrevocably forfeited the right to discharge their duties, and reiterated the baptism conferred by the heretics. Wiser and more merciful than the sectarians, who under various titles — Novatians, Montanists, Donatists, Luciferans—strove to enclose within narrow limits a society intended to embrace the whole of humanity and the entire world, the Church by her councils and her numerous acts has constantly offered pardon to repentant heretics, and has

[1] Epist. lviii. ad Paulinum, 10.   [2] Epist. ad Magnum, 5.

frequently restored to their hierarchial rank, bishops who had been momentarily led into heresy or constrained by violence. To the sophism of the deacon Hilarion, who had pertinaciously defended re-baptism, Jerome opposed from preference the custom of the Roman Church, as being more decisive than the contrary attempts of distinguished and saintly adversaries. "Cyprian sought to avoid polluted springs and untried waters; so as further to separate himself from them he condemned the baptism of heretics, and sent to Stephen the Pope, and the twenty-second successor of St Peter, the decree passed upon the subject by the Council of Africa. Cyprian's effort was fruitless. Later, the same bishops who, with the bishops of Carthage, unanimously had decreed the re-baptism of heretics, having reverted to the ancient custom, passed a fresh decree."[1] Other Popes, Julius, Mark and Sylvester upheld in their turn this baptismal discipline, and the Council of Nicea solemnly proclaimed it.

Does not Jerome at times exceed in his polemical writings, does one not find in them cutting personalities, cunning arguments and pleasantries, which the austere good taste of a Bossuet or a Fénelon would have shrunk from? Did he not wish sometimes to prove too much, and for this very reason did he not succeed in provoking doubt and opposition?

The treatise written against Jovinianus, a traducer of Christian virginity, aroused much criticism even during the lifetime of its author. Jerome was accused

[1] Dial. adversus Luciferianos.

of having been too vehement in his depreciation of matrimony. Perhaps the picture which he drew of women towards the end of the first book, may remind the pertinacious student of the seventeenth century, too much of Boileau's famous satire, in which are mingled both the enfeebled inspiration of Juvenal and the accents of a sorrowful old age, and which Bossuet, although a friend of the poet's, censured so severely. This man has taken upon himself to blame women; he seems regardless as to whether he condemn marriage and estrange from it those to whom it was given as a remedy. . .[1] But there certainly is a wide gulf between the selfish, and after all, fallacious and morose celibacy, which the satiric poets lauded, and the devoted celibacy extolled by Jerome. If Jerome, however, was at times unduly influenced by his humour or disposition, if he painted his picture of feminine faults and vices in too sombre colours, the friend of Paula, Eustochium, Marcella, and many other noble virgins and matrons personally corrected the exaggerated character of his description in the enthusiastic eulogies he had shortly before bestowed upon various historic or fabulous heroines. As to the contempt for the marriage tie with which Jerome was accredited, he exonerated himself upon this point in an apologetic letter to Pammachius, in which he recalled that in the incriminated treatise he had proclaimed the legitimacy of marriage, and that he had steered an even course between the Jews and the Gentiles, who did not understand the virtue of perfect continence, and the Oriental sects,

[1] Treatise upon Concupiscence, chap. viii.

whose false spiritualism condemned all union between the sexes.

"As, cautious traveller, I warned my reader at almost every step that I regarded matrimony as lawful, although preferring the continence of widows and virgins to the married state, a wise and kindly reader would have interpreted those of my assertions which seemed to him unduly severe, by the context, and would not have accused me of having advanced contrary opinions in the same work. Does any writer exist, so stupid or so ignorant of his art, as to praise and censure the same thing, as to destroy that which he had built so as to rebuild that which he häd destroyed, and after having triumphed over his enemy to pierce himself with his own sword?"[1] Jerome, moreover, as he frequently asserted, merely repeated the teachings of his predecessors. And the polemical writer, confident in a doctrine which he had not originated, but which he had received, turned upon his adversaries in tones of vengeful irony. "Execrable crime," he cried, "the churches are ruined, the entire world has stopped its ears, so as not to hear me, because I have declared virginity to be more holy than matrimony." Jerome terminated his defence with an humble allusion to his past. "Finally, I protest that I have never condemned marriage—that I do not condemn it. I answered my adversary (Jovinianus), I have not feared the pitfalls which my own people might lay for me. I extol virginity to the skies, not that I possess it, but

[1] Epist. xlviii. ad Pammachium, 12.

because I admire above all a blessing which is no longer mine. To praise in others that wherein one is oneself deficient is a sincere and discreet avowal. The weight of my body holds me down upon the earth; is that a reason to admire the flight of the birds any the less? Should I not praise the dove which swiftly traverses space without even stirring its wings?"

The controversialist whom we have been studying frequently executed the work of an historian, for which he was fitted, to a certain extent at least, by his vast and accurate memory, and by his taste for erudite researches, and for which the eloquence with which he was naturally gifted did not disqualify him; who could complain of Sallust and Tacitus having been eloquent? Many pages from history are to be found in Jerome's polemical treatises; take, for instance, the description of the Council of Rimini and the narrative of the events which followed. "The ship of the apostles was in jeopardy, the tempest raged, the waves beat incessantly upon the sides of the boat. The Lord awoke and rebuked the wind and the raging of the waters; the monster (Constans) dies, and calm is restored. Through the indulgence of the new prince (Julian) all the bishops who had been banished from their sees are restored to their churches. Then did Egypt receive Athanasius as a conqueror, then did the church of Gaul greet Hilarion returning from the battle-field, with loud acclamations. At the return of Eusebius, bishop of Vercelli, Italy cast aside her mourning garments."[1] Jerome, the painter of this

Dialog. adversus Luciferianos, 19.

vivid picture, had planned a task of the same nature as that of Eusebius of Cæsarea. "I purpose," he says in the beginning of his "Life of St Malchus," "provided that God grant me the necessary time, and that my censors cease from persecuting a fugitive and a recluse, I purpose to relate how, and with the help of what men, from our Lord's advent up to the present day, the Church of Christ was born and developed. How it waxed mighty under persecution, and how it was crowned by martyrdom; how also when the emperors became Christian it lost in virtue what it had gained in wealth and in power."[1] Stern words to which many other ecclesiastical writers to whom the evils of their day were forcibly brought home have given utterance. After all, persecution, creating as it does formidable perils for the weak, who form the majority, is not the Church's normal condition. Surely the society instituted and governed by Jesus Christ is sufficiently strong—history has proved it—to face and to pass through, producing saints the while, the test of prosperity.

Jerome did not carry out his scheme, neither did he translate the Ecclesiastical History by Eusebius, which in handing down the story of the glorious sources of its origin has preserved for Christianity its titles of nobility. We owe to Jerome, however, the version of another of the Bishop of Cæsarea's works, namely the "Chronicle," the original of which has perished. Besides completing the somewhat meagre portions concerning Roman history, the translator continued this work from the twentieth

[1] Vita Malchi monachi captivi.

year of the reign of Constantine until the death of the Emperor Valens in 378.

This work, which in spite of its breaks and inaccuracies rendered great service during many years, dates from 388. A few years later, in 392, Jerome wrote his " De Viris Illustribus," which is the title he himself gave it,[1] although he has acknowledged that he should rather have entitled it " De Scriptoribus Ecclesiasticis."[2] This latter would perhaps have been a more appropriate title to a work in whose 135 chapters, according to the request of Dexter, the prefect of the Prætorium, are drawn up a catalogue of authors, all of whom, with the exception of Philo and Seneca, were Christians. Jerome even professed to discover disciples of Christianity in the Jew Alexandrinus and in the Spanish philosopher. A few heretics were also mentioned. Jerome began his list with the name of St Peter the Apostle, he closed it with his own. "I placed myself at the end of the volume," he wrote, " even I, a wretched abortion and the very last among Christians, and I deemed it necessary briefly to indicate all the works written by me up till the fourteenth year of the reign of Theodosius."[3]

One may criticise this book in which Athenagoras, the apologist, receives no mention, and where conciseness too frequently degenerates into dryness, yet in it some of Jerome's most eminent qualities are displayed. Evidences of his critical talent are discernible in his refusal to recognise the style of

---

[1] Epist. xlvii. ad Desiderium, 3.
[2] Epist. cxii. ad Augustinum, 3.
[3] Epist. xlvii. ad Desiderium, 3.

Minucius Felix in the treatise " De Fato," which was ascribed to the polished author of the Octavius. This work of Jerome's obtained a lasting success. Ébert says that " It serves as a foundation to later writers, and however imperfect it may be, it has none the less remained to us as an evidence of its author's immense erudition, and in many respects as a unique source of history and literature." [1]

Jerome has left us the biography of three hermits; we will first mention that of St Paul, the institutor of the eremitical life, described to us by Montalembert, who took this passage in his eloquent summary from Jerome: " Discovered by Anthony in his cave, overshadowed by the palm-tree which afforded him food and raiment, he offered him the hospitality which has been so often recorded in history and sung in verse, and died, bequeathing him the tunic of palm-leaves in which Anthony arrayed himself upon Easter Day and at Whitsuntide as with the armour of a hero who had passed away at the very moment of victory." [2]

It may be remembered that Jerome met, in the vicinity of Antioch, the monk Malchus, and it was from the mouth of this aged man who had at last entered upon the peace of the desert, that he heard the narrative of the strange adventures of which his biography is composed. The life of St Hilarion, which was also drawn from an oral source as well as from written documents — a letter from St

---

[1] Ébert. General history of the literature of the Middle Ages in Europe. Book ii., St Jerome.
[2] The Monks of the West. Book i. to vi.

Epiphanius is mentioned in the first chapter—covers more ground than the two other biographies. The ascetic of Bethlehem seems to have delighted in glorifying his daring contemporary who introduced monasticism into Palestine; he relates his penances and miracles; he follows him in his journeys to Egypt and Sicily, to the Island of Cyprus, where Hilarion expired at the age of eighty, addressing the following joyful exhortation to his soul: " Speed forth, oh my soul, what fearest thou ? After serving Christ for nigh upon seventy years wouldst thou shrink affrighted from death ? " [1]

In this cursory review of the works of St Jerome, his letters, which have however been freely and frequently quoted, and whose ample and attractive matter would well repay study, have not yet been mentioned. M. Ébert has divided these letters into six categories. First, those in which Jerome relates incidents of his own life and of the life of others, then what the Saint termed consolatory letters, " Scripsi consolatoriam (epistolam) de morte filiae ad Paulam "; funeral orations (Epitaphia); letters of exhortation (the title is Jerome's); polemical apologetic letters in which the author both defends and attacks; and finally the didactic letters, such as the fifty-seventh letter to Pammachius, in which last class M. Ebert includes the *exegetical* letters.

" St Jerome," says this author, " first gave the true model of the modern epistolary style; his individuality never revealed itself under more remarkable and varied aspects than in his corres-

[1] Vita Sancti Hilarionis Eremitae, 45.

pondence. The collection of his letters was the delight of the Middle Ages, the world at the time of the Reformation still revelled in them."[1]

Erasmus, an ardent admirer of St Jerome, whose command of language he had the temerity to compare with that of Cicero, was one of the most enthusiastic panegyrists of this correspondence, which he would willingly have commentated. "Flagrat jam olim mihi incredibili ardore animus Hieronymianas Epistolas Commentario illustrandi," he wrote. The eminent humanist exceeded all limits when in his reaction against the scholastic he complained of the sensation which Albert the Great and Duns Scotus, for whom we are more just than he, were creating in the schools. (Scotus, Albertus et his impolitiores auctores omnibus in scholis perstrepent.") But he was fully justified when he pleaded that the hermit of Bethlehem should also be listened to, and when he demanded that the eloquent defender of the teachings of Christianity should be accorded a prominent place.

Jerome's letters afford us pleasure for the same reason that they delighted our forbears. We see the scenes which they put before us, for example the description of the invasion of the Huns, in a letter to Oceanus, Fabiola's funeral oration; in another letter, the picture of the desert island whither Bonosus, the friend of his younger days, had retired. "Bonosus," he wrote to Rufinus, with whom he was then still on affectionate terms,

[1] History of the literature of the Middle Ages in Europe Book ii., St Jerome.

"thy friend and mine is ascending the prophetic ladder of Jacob's dream, he bears his cross, gives no thought to the morrow, and looks not backward. He sows in tears so that he may reap in joy. .
The truth of such a miracle surpasses all the wonders invented by the poets of Greece and Rome. A youth of honourable family, who received the same literary education as you and I, distinguished among his contemporaries by reason of his rank and wealth, abandons his mother, his sisters, and a tenderly cherished brother, to land upon an island, upon whose shores, fertile in shipwreck, the sounding waves expend their fury, and which presents nought to the eye but jagged rocks and barren deserts. He at once establishes himself as though in a Paradise. No labourer, no monk, not even the young Onesimus, whom thou knowest, and whom he loved like a brother, shares his solitude in this vast wilderness. He is alone, or rather he is not alone, for Christ is with him, and he contemplates the glory of God which the apostles saw only in the desert. He discovers no tower-strengthened towns, but he has caused his name to be inscribed upon the roll of the new and eternal city. His limbs shiver under a wretched hair shirt, but thus arrayed he will the sooner penetrate the clouds and meet his Christ. He cannot hearken to the flow of pleasant fountains, but he drinks the waters which gush from the Saviour's side. An angry sea moans about the island, and the waves break with a crash upon its treacherous reefs. On land there is no verdure,

no luxuriant foliage casting shade upon the fields. Rocks stand sentinel upon every side, and the island is as if imprisoned. But Bonosus, calm, intrepid, guided with the arms of which the apostle has spoken, in his constant perusal of the Holy Scriptures, discerns the voice of God, and communes with Him in his prayers; perhaps some vision may appear to him upon his rock-bound island, as it did to John, when relegated to Patmos." [1]

Like our predecessors we read in these letters, which date from 370 to 419, the annals of half a century, and as M. Ébert observes, "we find in them a most interesting portrait-gallery, and a picture, which from the point of view of the civilisation of that epoch is invaluable." In these letters a procession of personages, some famous, others obscure, continually pass before us; an allusion to a few of them would not be amiss. Without mentioning those women, Paula, Eustochium, Marcella, and many others who were valiant even unto heroism, and who form such an incomparable escort to Jerome's name in history, notable among his correspondents were Pope Damasus, Augustine of Hippo, Chromatius of Aquilea, Heliodorus, and Paulinus of Nola, whom Jerome, in an eloquent letter, exhorted to the study of the holy works, saying: "I ask you, beloved brother, to live in the midst of all these things" (revealed to us by the Scriptures) "to meditate upon them, to know and to seek nought else; does it not seem as if this were beginning here below the life of heaven? Do

[1] Epist. iii. ad Rufinum Monachum.

not take exception to the simplicity of the Scriptures and to the unpolished language, which betokens either a mistake of the translator or the intention of the pious author, who wished to make himself understood by the vulgar, and in the same discourse instruct both the learned and the ignorant. I do not flatter myself that I understand everything in the Scriptures, and that I am able to gather upon this terrestrial plane the fruits of a tree whose roots are in heaven; still I confess it is this for which I yearn. To one who has not yet begun to walk I offer myself, not as a master but as a companion; to him who asks is given, to him who knocks is opened, he who seeks finds. Let us acquire upon earth, knowledge which will stand us in good stead in heaven." [1]

In another letter Jerome, after having praised the learning and the talent of Paulinus, again said to him: "To this learning, to this eloquence, add the study and understanding of the Scriptures and thou wilt soon surpass us all. Gird, then, I beg of thee, thy loins for toil, for life gives nothing to mortals except at the cost of arduous labour. Be illustrious in the Church as thou wert in the Senate. Amass spiritual treasures which thou canst daily pour forth. May these spiritual riches never fail thee now that thou art in the prime of life, and may thy hair not yet grow white. In thee nothing mediocre will content me: to see thee in the foremost rank; to see thee perfect, is my ambition." [2]

These letters, in which fifty years of political and religious history are vividly revived, and which evoke

[1] Epist. liii. 9.   [2] Epist. lviii. ad Paulinum 11.

so many and such varied characters, are interesting in still another respect, namely, in the fact that they reveal Jerome to us, better than any of his other works. A correspondence is generally the true portrait and history of a soul, and when this soul has been a noble one, when to express noble sentiments it has found eloquence, we can but delight in reading the history and in contemplating the portrait which it has left us of itself in the pages of a correspondence frequently written from day to day. That is why we revert with pleasure to Jerome's letters, at least to certain of Jerome's letters. That also is the secret of the fascination which St Augustine's correspondence exercises over those who have once tasted of its living fountains, which give forth both tenderness and doctrine. We experience a similar and even more penetrating charm, for we are on more familiar ground, when we reopen the correspondence of Father Lacordaire, especially the letters to Madame Swetchine, from those written in anxious and troublous times to the letter dated the 30th of September 1856, in which we see the restorer of the Dominican Order in France in the serene glory of twilight, "like an aged lion who has journeyed in the deserts, and who, in majestic repose, contemplates with a somewhat melancholy air the sea and its waves."

The lion recalls us to St Jerome, whose doctrine we have still to briefly expound, although it is always a matter of some doubt whether in the proper acceptation of the word St Jerome may be said to have had a doctrine.

CHAPTER II

THE DOCTRINE OF ST JEROME

AS the word is applied to the teachings of St Anselm and St Thomas, or to those of St Augustine, Jerome had no doctrine. The bishop of Hippo, his contemporary, broached, either to expose or to defend them, almost every point of revealed doctrine, several of which he presented synthetically; he essayed explanations and opened points of view of every description, leaving them as an inheritance to his successors, and thus justifying the remark of Charles de Rémusat, an able historian who wrote: "One can scarcely realise to what an extent this great mind, so cultivated and so polished, has furnished ideas and studies to the scholars of our own times" (the eleventh and twelfth centuries). "Before ascribing the invention of a system or the understanding of an ancient thought to any of them, one should first ascertain that St Augustine has said nothing upon the subject."[1]

All these masters, St Bonaventura, St Thomas, St Anselm, and St Augustine before them, were the mighty architects of the doctrinal development and dogmatic progress of which I have said elsewhere—my readers must pardon me if I quote my own words:

[1] St Anselm, p. 476.

"Not only did theological language gain greater precision and acquire a delicacy, firmness, and vigour which satisfy the subtlest requirements of the Christian soul and disconcert and refute all the presumptions of heresy; not only are the data of the Revelation successively divulged, thanks especially to the infallible authority which, to quote the words of St Vincent of Lérins, completes the unfinished passages, consolidates and confirms what is already expressed, and retains with loving care what is already confirmed and defined. But the catholic intellect penetrates still further into the essence of revealed dogma, gains greater insight into its beauties, and the better grasps its harmonious proportions and its relations to the doctrinal whole, as well as to the aspirations of human nature; finally, following the example of doctors too great to be accused of temerity, it strives to discover and if possible to make manifest its most hidden meaning. As St Anselm said: 'It is faith seeking, and frequently meeting, intellect.'"[1]

It is true that one must not expect from Jerome either a synthetic exposition of doctrine, or views which treat of profound dogmatical subjects. It would be a more difficult task to write a theology of St Jerome than a theology of St Anselm, St Thomas or St Bonaventura.

It is possible, however, to gather and to recapitulate the doctrine scattered among the works of the great anchorite. This has been done by Dom Remy Ceillier, the author of the "General History of Ecclesiastical and Sacred Writers," who, step by step,

[1] Conferences upon the faith, p. 316, 317.

follows Jerome upon every point of Catholic teaching, first setting forth his views upon the inspiration and the canon of the Scriptures. He acknowledges that the learned exegete did not consider those books of the ancient Testament which do not figure in the Jewish canon, as inspired. It has already been said that the Church pronounced to the contrary, and the decree of Trent—not to mention the decrees of the council of Hippo and Carthage, and the letter of the pope, St Innocent I., to St Exuperus of Toulouse—fixed in its catalogue the position of the books which Jerome had doubted. The hesitations and even the denials of a doctor, no matter how famous he may have been, will never shake the faith of a Catholic. Doubtless should the faithful wish to assure themselves of the truth of our beliefs, more especially should they wish to defend it, they will search the monuments of the past and discover in the works of the fathers, even the most ancient, not only the dogma of an infallible Church which embraces all other tenets, but a startling manifestation of many other dogmas, such as, for example, that of the Eucharist. They will convince themselves that whatever may have been the divergences of certain churches upon certain questions, moral universality was never the character of the sentiments opposed to those which were later to be defined. And as the authority of an ever-living Church is the guiding rule of their faith, they will not be astonished, still less scandalised, by the divergences which their studies will have disclosed to them; they will believe in the validity of baptism conferred by heretics, in spite of the protests of St Cyprian; and in spite of St Jerome's doubts, they will believe in the inspiration of the deuterocanonical books of the Old Testament. It is curious to notice how often the traditional and Catholic meaning has triumphed in Jerome's mind and in his speech over the objections of the critic. "He frequently employed the deuterocanonical books," wrote the Abbé Tronchon, "he called the book of Ecclesiasticus a Divine writing. He quotes the book of Wisdom as scripture, and uses it with other texts of the protocanonical works as having an equal value. In his commentaries upon the Epistle to the Galatians, he quotes in succession a verse from the book of Wisdom, one from the Epistle to the Romans, one from the first Epistle to the Corinthians, and a deuterocanonical verse from Daniel. He employs the testimony of the deuterocanonical parts of Daniel, which he cites as belonging to this prophet's book, in his refutation of the Pelagians, and explains the meaning of the passages which the latter were doing their best to render obscure. In his commentary upon the prophet Nahum he proved by another deuterocanonical verse from Daniel, and upon the authority of Ezekiel, that Israel was called the race of Canaan, because of her crimes." [1]

As to the books of the New Testament, Jerome held as inspired those, which in spite of partial and temporary doubts, tradition has declared to be such, and which the Church has inscribed upon its canon. Interested in all the works which, apart from cur-

[1] The Holy Bible. General Introduction, 3rd part, p. 149.

THE DOCTRINE OF SAINT JEROME

rent tradition, were the growth of popular memory and imagination, always so easily imposed upon, Jerome made a translation, no longer extant, of the Aramean Gospel according to the Jews which Remy Ceillier believed to be an alteration of the first gospel, although Mr Harnack declares that its author had never heard of St Matthew or of St Luke. Jerome was careful not to compare this gospel, of which his writings have preserved us a few extracts, with our canonical gospel.

He countenanced the Epistle which bears the name of St Barnabas, and the "Shepherd" of Hermas, but sternly condemned apocryphal works such as the Acts, the Gospel and the Apocalypse of Saint Peter, one book of Ecclesiastes, and another of Judgment, and also the journeys of St Paul and St Thecla.

As to the veracity of the Holy Books—the denial of which would also demolish the dogma of Scriptural inspiration—without entering upon a delicate hermeneutical question, we will merely repeat an opinion more than once expressed by Jerome. Speaking of a text in Jeremiah, he finds fault with the Septuagint for not having given, as in the original, the title of prophet to Hananiah, who was no prophet, "as if," he argued, "there were not many things in the Scriptures which were recorded according to the opinion of the times, and not according to the true state of things (quasi non multa in Scripturis sanctis dicantur juxta opinionem illius temporis quo gesta referuntur et non juxta quod rei veritas continebat)." Jerome put the same construction upon the 15th verse, of which the sacred text ran thus: "The prophet Jeremiah said unto the prophet Hananiah: Hear now, Hananiah: The Lord hath not sent thee. And the prophet died (Et dixit Jeremias ad Hananiam prophetam: Audi, Hanania: non misit te Dominus. Et Mortuus est propheta)."[1] Jerome observed that the original Hebrew version persisted in calling Hananiah prophet, and asked how the sacred writer could have applied the name of prophet to a man whom he denies having been sent by God ("Quomodo enim prophetam poterat appellare quem missum a Domino denegabat?"). This is the context of his answer: "As we have already said, the truth and order of history was in this case preserved by the transcription, not of the reality, but of the general opinion of the times (. Historiæ veritas et ordo servatur, sicut prædiximus, non juxta id quod erat, sed juxta quod illo tempore putabatur)."

In another instance, speaking of the verse in St Matthew, "and the King was sorry" (at the petition of the daughter of Herodias, who asked for the head of John the Baptist), Jerome, who did not believe that Herod's grief was sincere, made this observation: "It was customary in the Scriptures, for the historian to record the opinion of the majority, such as it was then generally admitted (Consuetudinis Scripturarum est opinionem multorum sic narret historicus, quomodo eo tempore ab omnibus credebatur"). Exegetes and apologists of the present day profess to have discovered in this opinion of a

[1] xxviii. 10.

THE DOCTRINE OF SAINT JEROME

Father, considered by the Encyclical *Providentissimus Deus* to be unequalled as an expounder of the Bible (Hieronymus a singulari Bibliorum scientia magnisque ad eorum usum laboribus nomine Doctoris maximi præconio Ecclesiæ est honestatus), a principle of solution to the obstacles which, in the name of history, are raised against certain Biblical facts. In the assertion of facts of a physical order, the sacred writer frequently adjusted his language to obvious appearances; a method taught by St Augustine and St Thomas, and with supreme authority by Pope Leo XIII.; why, therefore, should we not believe that in the statement of facts concerning history, the sacred writer occasionally spoke from certain appearances which were equivalent to obvious appearances? Historical facts, when, as is sometimes the case, handed down by an erroneous tradition founded upon deceptive appearances, assume an aspect which does not correspond with the reality; but the populace, who have neither the leisure nor the intellect necessary to reach the bottom of things, holds by what strikes it, judging from the outside, and forming its opinion and language upon exterior evidences and appearances. The exegetes and apologists who refer to St Jerome, assert that it is quite permissible to record history according to popular opinion, in a work intended not for the historical but for the religious and moral instruction of the people, to record it, either indicating the reference in the Scriptures to popular opinion as in the verse from Jeremiah which has been lately quoted (Et dixit Jeremias ad Hananiam... Non misit te Dominus), or even without any such indication, at least of an explicit character, as in the text from St Matthew. It is no deception to oneself or to others, in writing the current opinion, to give only what one wishes of it, and in this manner of writing there is nothing contrary to the infallibility and plenary inspiration proclaimed in the Encyclical of the 18th of November 1893.

We have dwelt at length upon St Jerome's scriptural opinions, and must now proceed to the examination of other doctrines professed by the illustrious recluse. It is scarcely necessary to prove that upon all dogmas of which the Church preserves the inalienable heritage—natural dogmas which she has restored, and supernatural dogmas which her apostles revealed to the world—Jerome professed an irreproachable doctrine. He believed in Providence, and the apparent confusion of human affairs was powerless to shake his soul's faith in a Paternity supremely wise and supremely loving.

"A host of burning questions cause a tumult in my soul," he cried, as he stood before the grave into which Blesilla's corpse had just been lowered. " I wonder why godless old age is permitted to enjoy the advantages of the century; why innocent youth, why sinless childhood are cut down in their budding springtime; why children of two and three, new-born babes still at the breast, are possessed by devils, struck with leprosy or epilepsy, whilst the godless, the adulterers, the homicides and the sacrilegious, resplendent with health, blaspheme against God ? Yet the iniquity of the father does not descend upon the son; only he who has sinned shall die. And even if the ancient decree were still in existence, does it not seem unjust that the son should expiate the sins of the father? Does it not seem unjust that the debts accumulated during a long life by a sinful parent should be paid by a sinless child? And I said, ' It is then in vain that I have kept my heart pure, and cleansed my hands amongst the innocent, that I have been daily sore tormented, and that every morning has brought me fresh trials and afflictions!'" Jerome, however, did not dwell long upon these painful questions, to which so many weak and troubled souls have found no answer but in rebellion; he hastened to add: "As these thoughts were passing through my mind, I received this lesson from the Prophet:[1] I had undertaken to penetrate these mysteries, and until I had entered into God's sanctuary and had seen what shall be the end of the wicked, the burden of my task weighed heavily upon me. The divine judgments are impenetrable. Oh, fathomless treasure of the wisdom and knowledge of God. Inscrutable are the decrees of the Lord, impenetrable are His ways. God is good, therefore all His decrees must be good also. Should I suffer bereavement through the death of a spouse, I would weep; but since God has so willed it, I would suffer with a resigned heart. An only son is ravished from me: the blow is a terrible one but I shall bear it bravely —for the God who took my son from me is the same God who gave him to me. Should I become blind, the reading of a friend shall be a consolation unto

[1] Exod. xxxiv.

me. Should my ears, succumbing to deafness, fail me, I shall the more easily abstain from sin, and think but of God. Should dire poverty, cold, sickness, nakedness, be my lot, I will await death as the supreme end to my sufferings which, since they will be replaced by ultimate bliss, I shall not consider long. Let us not forget the lesson in this verse of the Psalms—' Thou art just, O Lord, and thy judgments are equitable.'

"Words like these can only be spoken by one who, in the midst of tribulation, glorifies the Lord, and, believing himself alone responsible for his adversities, finds in them cause to glorify the Divine clemency. . When in good health I devoutly thank the Lord. In sickness I bless the divine will which has subjected me to probation. . . In my weakness I am strong, saith the apostle. The soul's vitality is strengthened by the anguish of the flesh. Paul in his sufferings cried upon God to succour him, but God answered him: My grace is sufficient to thee, for weakness fosters strength. To restrain the temptation to pride which might have sprung from these very revelations, a monitor was given to Paul to remind him of human frailties, like the slave who stood behind the victorious general upon his triumphal chariot, and, in the midst of the acclamations of the people, kept repeating to him, ' Remember that thou art but human. '"[1]

Jerome did not only testify to the truths and mysteries of purely rational theodicy, upon which revealed doctrine has thrown so much light, but he

---

[1] Epist. xxxix., ad Paulam.

was also a staunch champion of dogmas of the supernatural order. It is true that we should not expect from him a treatise upon that most sublime mystery of Christianity, the Trinity, like the masterly work in which Augustine, in the prime of life and at the height of his genius, united a doctrinal exposition, which subsequent scholastic works have further specified, with ingenious explanatory essays founded upon psychological observations. Still, is it necessary to be a metaphysician or a psychologist to uphold the Trinitarian dogma? "Who would be sacrilegious enough," queried Jerome, "to maintain that there are three substances in God? There is in God one unique nature which subsists veritably. For what subsists veritably does not derive its being from elsewhere, but possesses it in itself. All that is created seems to be, but, in the full sense of the word, is not; for there was a time when things created were nonexistent, and that which has had a beginning may also have an end. To God alone, who is eternal, that is, who has had no beginning, may properly be applied the name of essence. . Thus there is in God one substance and three consubstantial persons, perfect, equal and co-eternal. . ."[1]

All things are one to the Father and to the Son. A disciple of Gregory Nazianzen, Jerome professed upon the third person of the Trinity the same doctrines as did his master. "All that appertains to the Father and to the Son appertains also to the Holy Ghost. When the Holy Ghost is sent, he is sent by the Father and by the Son. In various parts of the

[1] Epist. xv. ad Damasum Papam 4.

Scriptures he is called the Spirit of God the Father, and the Spirit of Jesus Christ. This is why it is written in the Acts of the Apostles, that those who had only been baptised by John, and who believed in God the Father and in Jesus Christ, but who ignored the very existence of the Holy Ghost, were baptised anew; and this second baptism was the true one, for without the Holy Ghost there is no Trinity." [1]

The texts in which Jerome asserted the Incarnation of the Word, and in which he combated the heresies which strove to divide the one and divine person of Jesus Christ, were plentiful and decisive. " Jesus Christ was crucified as man, He is glorified as God. . We do not express ourselves thus, being convinced that in Jesus Christ, other would be the God, other would be the man. We do not introduce two persons in the only Son of God as we are accused of doing. In our Saviour's words there are certain things which relate to the glory of His divinity, and others which concern our salvation. It was for us that He took upon Himself the form and the nature of a slave, and forced Himself to be obedient until death—the death of the cross. And the Word became flesh and dwelt among us." [2]

None have more vigorously supported the dogmas of the divine maternity, and the perpetual virginity of Mary, than Jerome, whose struggles against Helvidius and Jovinianus are already known to us. Jerome supported and defended the doctrines of free-will,

[1] Epist. cxx. ad Hedibiam, cap. ix.   [2] *Ibid.*

THE DOCTRINE OF SAINT JEROME

original sin, and divine mercy, and waged war against all those who contested their veracity. His last battle was fought against the Pelagians. Jerome would not have permitted Baïus and Jansenius to claim him as an ancestor any more than would have his friend St Augustine. "God," he said, "has ordained possible things, but it is not men who render them possible. We are all dependent upon God, and have need of His mercy."[1]

The relentless dogma of reprobation prior to the prevision of sin, was odious to Jerome. "Do I desire the death of a sinner," asked our Lord, "do I not rather wish him to turn from his wickedness and live? For such is the will of God that all shall be saved and come to the knowledge of the truth."[2] The number is too great of those who have perished "because they have refused to believe and have offended against the Holy Ghost. . God wished to save all those who desired salvation, and has led them to salvation so that they might by their own will deserve the reward. It is not His fault if some have been unwilling to believe. In coming into the world His will was that all should believe and save themselves."[3]

Upon the sacraments which are the means of grace, Jerome professed the same doctrine which is taught in the Church. It is unnecessary to repeat all that he has said in praise of the divine institution of baptism, but we have quoted one of

---

[1] Dialog. adversus Pelagianos. Lib. iii. 3.
[2] Commentar in Ezechielem. Lib. v., cap. xviii., v. 23.
[3] Commentar in Isaiam. Lib. xvii.

the many passages in his commentaries and in his letters, in which he upholds the dogma of the actual presence. In an epistle to Hedibia, who, from the extremities of Gaul, had appealed to him for instruction, he wrote: "You ask how these words of our Lord should be interpreted: Verily, I say unto you. I will drink no more of the fruit of the vine until that day that I drink it new with you in my Father's kingdom. Upon this passage some people have founded the fable of the millennium, during which they pretend that Jesus Christ will reign in the flesh upon the earth, and that He will drink of the wine of which He had not drunk until then. . But let us understand that the bread which the Lord broke and gave to His disciples was the body of our Lord and Saviour, as He assured His disciples when He said to them, 'Take, eat, this is my body; likewise the cup; Drink ye all of this, for this is my blood of the New Testament, which is shed for many. . .' If, therefore, the bread which descended from heaven is the body of our Lord, and if the wine which He gave to His disciples is the blood of the New Testament which was shed for many, for the remission of their sins, let us reject the Jewish fables, and go up with the Lord into the guest chamber; let us there receive the cup of the New Testament from His hands, make our Easter celebration, and draw from the divine beverage a holy rapture. . . . It was not Moses who gave us the Bread of Life, but Jesus Christ, who was both the guest and the feast, who partook Himself, and was partaken of. It is His blood which we drink. . ."[1] We should also read this passage from a commentary upon St Paul, in which Jerome speaks of the incomprehensible and bountiful mystery which ever sustains the fruitful vitality of the Church. "Between the show-bread (of the ancient law) and the body of Christ, there is as great a difference as between the shadow and the body, the image and the reality, the symbols of future things and the things themselves which the symbols represented. And just as gentleness, temperance and disinterestedness should be the most prominent virtues of a bishop, raising him above the laity, so also should he possess chastity and, so to speak, sacerdotal modesty, in order that the soul who administers the body of Christ should not only abstain from any act of impurity, but should also keep strict guard over his thoughts and glance."[2]

Jerome believed in sacrifice, as he did in the Eucharistic sacrament. "It is the fruit of the true vine which we daily press in our sacrifices," he wrote to Hedibia. "Our mystery," he said again, "is typified in these words—Thou art a priest for ever after the order of Melchisedec; we no longer immolate victims who have lost their reason as did Aaron, but we offer the bread and the wine, that is the body and the blood of Christ."[3] It was at Jerome's suggestion that Paula and Eustochium wrote to Marcella from Bethlehem: "Turn back as far as Genesis and you will see that the King of Salem . . . in the

---

[1] Epist. xx. ad Hedibiam.
[2] Commentar. in Ep. ad Titum.
[3] Commentar. in Ep. ad Titum.

image of Christ, offered the bread and the wine, and inaugurated the Christian sacrament of the body and blood of the Lord."[1]

Jerome also upheld the existence of a sacramental rite which gives remission to sins committed after baptism, and considered bishops and priests to be the ministers of forgiveness. "God forbid," he wrote to Heliodorus, "that I should speak ill of priests. They hold the keys to the kingdom of heaven, and possess the power of judging to a certain extent, before the day of Judgment. ."[2] He has made another allusion elsewhere to the power which the divine mercy confers upon bishops and priests, whom he warns in the stern tones which were customary to him, against pride and despotism.[3]

It is doubtful, however, whether Jerome, in spite of his frequent allusions to the prerogatives of priesthood, ever consented to realise the great difference between the priest and the bishop, which the Catholic teachings proclaim, and whether, instead of regarding the episcopacy as a divine institution, he did not consider it a purely ecclesiastical institution. Does he not seem thus to have paved the way to the Protestants and the Rationalists, who in the second century rejected in certain churches, whose example other churches followed, the establishment of monarchical, or what is termed uninominal Episcopacy? Indeed, he said

[1] Epist. xlvi. Paulæ et Eustochii ad Marcellam 7.
[2] Epist. xiv. ad Heliodorus 8.
[3] Commentar. in Matt. Lib. iii., cap. xvi., v. 19.

in his commentary upon the Epistle to Titus that originally the churches were governed in common by a college of priests, but that in order to put a check upon rivalry and to avoid schism, it was decreed that the supremacy over all the churches should be confided to one.[1] He expressed the same opinions in a letter to Evangelus.[2]

It should be noticed that in this letter, after rebuking the arrogance of the Roman deacons who, proud of the riches of the Supreme Church of which they were the dispensers, held themselves above the priests, Jerome, in order effectually to suppress this arrogant spirit, adopted a polemical method too frequently resorted to, rushed to the opposite extreme and very nearly declared the ordinary priests to be equal to bishops. I say nearly, because I have found in the same letter a direct confession of this opinion. "Always excepting ordination, does a bishop do anything which a priest does not do also?" But it is this right to ordain, to transmit to others the divine power of priesthood or even of Episcopacy which constitutes the peerless dignity of a bishop; for from whom can such a right directly emanate except from Him who instituted the sacraments and endowed them with a sanctifying power.

The Reverend Father De Smedt, whose words upon the subject we would do well to read, has observed that "in the Dialogus Contra Luciferianos, c. 9, St Jerome seems to trace the pre-eminence of

---

[1] Commentar. in Epist. ad Titum. Cap. I., v. 5.
[2] Epist. cxlvi. ad Evangelum 1.

bishops over ordinary priests, to a divine or at least to an apostolic institution. . He seems to represent the prerogatives of the Episcopal rank as an essential principle of the order and the unity of the Church. He attributes one of these privileges, the power of confirmation, to the descent of the Holy Ghost upon the Apostles at Pentecost, which certainly seems to prove that they must have been recognised from the very beginning. It seems to me that from this we can pretty much conclude that Jerome had no very definite idea upon the subject." [1]

This conclusion, expressed by a master, is sufficient, and we must acknowledge that upon the point in question Jerome hesitated. It is the special right of the Church canonically to explain all controversies. Should we wish to find the clue to the objections which Jerome raised to the origin of Episcopacy, we might read these words of that eminent Bollandist writer. "Catholic theologians, although maintaining as is their usual custom that the Episcopacy is an order distinct from that of the ordinary priests and was divinely ordained, need, however, have no scruple in admitting that this institution did not reach its complete development and take its definite shape until after the time of the Apostles. So long as the Apostles were alive, the Church possessed in them a visible and a living authority. There is nothing to prevent thinking it possible that the Apostles always kept the government of the Churches in their own hands, being substituted by

[1] Review of historical subjects, 1st Oct. 1888. The organisation of the Christian Churches until the middle of the Third Century.

what we term ordinary priests for the usual practices and for certain particular functions of the administration. ." In point of fact, however, the most ancient Churches, dating back as far as the lifetime of the Apostles, were governed by the Episcopacy, and what has been called the Unitarian Episcopacy. James was bishop of Jerusalem. In the pastoral epistles we read of Timothy and Titus being charged through their Episcopal rights with the government of the Churches. And finally, as the Rev. Father De Smedt has observed, "the warnings which (in the Apocalypse) were successively given to the *Angel* of each of the Seven Churches evidently referred to one individual person bearing the weight and the responsibility of the supreme administration."

It was a vital question with Jerome, as it is with us all, to know which was the Church founded by Christ, and to know also what were the distinguishing characteristics enabling us to recognise it. The true and only Church was founded upon St Peter. The testimony which Jerome, in a letter to Damasus, rendered to the Roman supremacy has already been quoted; here, however, is another testimony of the same nature. The following words were attributed by Jerome to Jovinianus, who, anxious to depreciate the virtues of virginity, recalled the fact that the supremacy was conferred upon a married man, and not upon John the virgin apostle; the truth of which Jerome did not contest but rather admitted, since he explained that by reason of his youth John was less fitted to receive the signal favour than Peter, who had reached a mature age.

"The Church is founded upon Peter," said Jerome, "although it has been said that it is also founded upon the apostles, all of whom received the keys of the heavenly kingdom, and that the solidarity of the Church is equally established upon them all, nevertheless one is chosen from amongst them in order that the unity of one leader might prevent any occasion for schism."[1] This Church which is one, is Apostolic. "I will speak my thoughts openly: we must abide in this Church which, having been founded on the apostles, endures until now."[2] This Church is catholic, it enfolds or calls all nations into its mighty unity, and we should not try as did Lucifer of Cagliari to restrict it to Sardinia. It is holy, but its holiness does not exclude sinners; all who have been baptised and have not left it through heresy, or who have not been excommunicated, belong to it. "As St Peter has said, the ark of Noah is the symbol of the Church. . . As there were in the ark every variety of animal, so there are in the Church men of all nations and customs. As there were in the ark leopards, goats, wolves, and lambs, so there are in the Church the just and the unjust, the vessels of gold and of silver mingled with the vessels of wood and of clay."[3] How merciful is this doctrine which the Church has persistently defended against a powerful spirit of pharisaism, and which Father Lacordaire so delighted in:

[1] Adversus Jovinianum. Lib. i. 26.
[2] Dialog. Adversus Luciferianos 28.
[3] Dialog. Adversus Luciferianos 22.

"How I have always loved," wrote the distinguished Dominican in his third letter upon the Christian life, "the admirable economy which has made the portals through which one enters into the city of God, so lofty and so wide, and the doors through which one departs from it, so low and so narrow. Wretched sectarians have repeatedly attempted to condemn sinners, and to discard them from the bosom of the Church; but the Church, faithful to her master's teachings and example, has ever retained them in her inmost recesses. ."

To pursue our investigation upon the rest of Jerome's doctrines. His letters and his controversial treatises have justified and precognised the invocation of Saints, the worship of the Cross and the worship of relics. "The day will come," he once wrote to Heliodorus in a transport of pious enthusiasm, "when triumphant thou shalt enter the New Jerusalem and share thy citizenship with Paul. Then also wilt thou beseech the same rights for those dear to thee, and pray for me who helped thee to conquer."[1] "If the apostles and martyrs, while still in the flesh and while occupied with their own salvation, can nevertheless pray for others," wrote Jerome to Vigilantius, "how much more will they be able to do so after they have won their crowns, their triumphs, and their victories."[2]

Man instinctively clings to every object which reminds him of the dear ones whom he has lost. Every trace of their earthly life, especially any writings, should they have left any, has the power to

[1] Epist. xiv. ad Heliodorum.   [2] Lib. contra Vigilantium 6.

prolong their presence, even to the very faintest tones of their voices, upon this earth. Respect and admiration sometimes produce the same effect as affection. "I have found," wrote Jerome, "Origen's twenty-five commentaries upon the twelve (minor) prophets, transcribed by the hand of the martyr Pamphilius, and in my joy at possessing them, in the care with which I preserved them, I seemed to myself master of the riches of Crœsus. If there is so much joy in the possession of a solitary letter written by a martyr, how much more is there in the possession of numerable pages in which one can almost see traces of his blood."[1]

Some secret instinct seemed to move Jerome unhesitatingly to accept the doctrine of the worship of relics, to which these words of J. de Maistre so particularly apply. "There is no dogma in the Catholic Church, no general usage belonging to exalted discipline even, which has not its roots in the inmost depths of human nature."[2] Enlightened by the Catholic teachings, Jerome was able to affirm and explain his adhesion to the cult of relics, in a letter to the Spanish priest Riparius, an adversary of Vigilantius. "We do not adore the relics of the martyrs, neither do we adore the sun, the moon, the archangels, the cherubim, or seraphim . for fear of rendering supreme worship to the creation instead of to the Creator, who is blessed throughout all centuries. We honour the relics of martyrs only to adore Him to whom they rendered the testimony of

[1] De Viris Illustribus, lxxv.
[2] Of the Pope. Book 3, chap. iii.

blood. We honour the servants so that the homage which we tender them may ascend to the Lord who said: Whoso receiveth you receiveth me. Whenever we enter the basilica of the apostles, of the prophets, and of the martyrs, are we bringing our homage to idolatrous temples? Are then the tapers which we light before the tombs of the Saints, signs of idolatry?"[1]

Jerome was no less explicit in his views upon the worship of the cross. It is he who has told us how fervently Paula venerated the instrument of salvation and how her dying lips formed its saving sign. It was he who commended Eustochium and Demetriade to fortify themselves with the sign of the cross, and he who has given us an account of how, with its help, the hermit Hilarion overcame the devil.

The problem of the final state of things, what is technically termed eschatology, rose before Jerome as it had before Origen, and as it does before every soul who has grasped the awful grandeur of human destiny. Knowing the answer which the Catholic faith has made to this question, it is natural to wonder whether Jerome's doctrine upon this point was always irreproachable. For a long time he had been so impregnated with the works of Origen, that even after he had vehemently shaken off the doctrinal authority of the distinguished Alexandrian, traces of Origenism may possibly have lingered in his mind. Have not many of our own contemporaries retained the impression of ideas which, with the best possible faith, they have amended

[1] Epist. cix. ad Riparium.

and have abjured, and does not their language sometimes betray a revival of the traditionalism of Lamenais, or of the fideism of the Abbé Bautain? Certain passages in Jerome's writings have given the impression that he doubted that, if the torments of the next world were not eternal, at least they must be so for all baptised sinners who have not died in incredulity, apostasy, or blasphemy. This, at all events, is the sense which a few portions of the commentary upon the sixty-third chapter of Isaiah, and the first book of the Dialogue against the Pelagians, seem to express. Vallarsi, the Italian editor of Jerome's works, tried to interpret these passages in an orthodox manner, but Ceillier, bishop of Avranches, Daniel Huet and Petau, refused to accept this favourable exegesis. If, however, Jerome betrays the influence of Origen in certain passages, there are many others in which, with his inflexible sternness, he maintained the Catholic doctrine. In commentating the third verse of the eleventh chapter of Ecclesiastes—" If the tree fall toward the south or toward the north, in the place where the tree falleth there it shall be" (Si ceciderit lignum ad austrum aut ad aquilonem, in quocumque loco ceciderit, ibi erit)—Jerome wrote "You are like unto this tree: no matter how long a life you may have, you cannot live for ever. Death like a mighty wind will uproot you, and in whatever direction you may fall, you will remain such as the last day of your life has found you, either hard and pitiless, or rich in mercy." In his commentary upon the Epistle to the Galatians, Jerome enumerated the various sins by which, accord-

THE DOCTRINE OF SAINT JEROME

ing to St Paul, man is excluded from the kingdom of God; the commentary upon the prophecy of Jonas also contains testimonies to the exegete's faith in the irrevocability of the sanction beyond the grave. He realised that the pity which would assure an unconditional pardon to all sins, except avowed infidelity, would be but a cruel kindness. The world, in its indulgence born of self-interest, readily absolves what it calls, and what we also, for want of a better word, will call sins of weakness; but it does not follow, however, that these sins are so trifling that they should be granted, so to speak, an unfailing pardon; for who can say how they sear the soul or souls, who can count the ruins which they have accumulated? All those who have not already done so, should read those bold and chaste pages in the "Knowledge of the Soul," in which Father Gratry describes the immense mischief caused by "playing with fire," or else those in which Charles Perraud, a disciple of Father Gratry, points out and denounces the excesses which have so frequently turned "the valley of tears into a sea of mire and blood." Unquestionably God pardons "sins of weakness," as He pardons sins of a graver nature resulting from rebellious pride, or from conscious malice, but He only pardons them in those who repent them with their tears. The pardon which the followers of Origen promise to souls which have been sinful until the end is offered by the divine clemency as long as the earthly struggle lasts, even at the very last hour, and is, let us hope, frequently accepted. So different from Father Ravignan in many respects, Jerome would certainly not have rejected this consoling thought of the pious monk, "At the last stage of the journey, upon the threshold of eternity, the mysteries of justice which take place within the soul are no doubt great, but the mysteries of mercy and of love are even greater."[1]

The hermit of Bethlehem was a champion of Catholic discipline, just as he was a champion of dogma. The Catholic discipline which was instituted for men of all races and all times has altered, as it was necessary that it should, and has been obliged to adapt itself to the varying needs of nations and of ages.

"Thou askest me," wrote Jerome to Lucinius the Spaniard, "whether thou shouldest fast upon Saturdays, and daily receive the Sacrament as is the custom in Rome or in Spain. . . I will answer thee briefly: when ecclesiastical traditions do not in any way run counter to the rules of faith, we should observe them in the same manner as we have received them from our predecessors, the practices of one particular Church not being prejudicial to those observed in another. . . Each province should hold its own opinions, and consider that the precepts of its forbears are laws descended from the apostles."[2]

This discipline which, during eighteen centuries, has adjusted itself to so many different exigencies, was no longer quite the same under Innocent III. as it had been under St Gregory the Great, and even at the present day is changing upon many points; but it has, however, remained intact in its outlines and in

[1] 36th Conference of Notre Dame.
[2] Epist. lxxi. ad Lucinium 7.

its early inspiration. It has maintained in the world, through its established institutions, the conception and the respect of the Christian ideal, the pursuit of which it has facilitated, and has raised barriers to arrest the waves of human covetousness.

It has established the great law of public prayer. Jerome tells us how this law was observed in his day, and the hours which he mentions as having been devoted to liturgical prayer seem to have been the same as those which, under the names of tierce, sexte, and none, we consecrate to this great duty. "There are," wrote the Saint, "three moments during the day when one should fall upon one's knees before God, namely, the third, the sixth, and the ninth hour, in accordance with the tradition of the Church. At the third hour the Holy Ghost descended upon the aposties at the sixth, Peter being hungry went up into the upper room to pray; and at the ninth, Peter and John went up together into the Temple."[1] While Jerome was writing these very lines, the office of Prime was being established in Palestine.[2] The Saint also tells us that the last hours of the day were sanctified by the singing of psalms, and that when the lamps were lit, they offered to God what the hermit termed the "Evening Sacrifice."[3]

Jerome has also given us information upon many other points, such as, for instance, upon the probable origin of Easter Eve: although our Lord did not

---

[1] Comment. in Daniel. Cap. vi., v. 10.
[2] Abbé Batifol. History of the Roman Breviary.
[3] Ep. cvii. ad Lætam 9.

indicate either the hour, the day, the season, or the period of his coming again (But pray that your flight be not in winter, neither on the Sabbath day [1]); although the apostles specified nothing upon the subject either, and although in his second epistle St Peter warned Christians against measuring the day of the Lord by the brief duration of their own, the faithful of the first generation expected that Jesus Christ would shortly reappear among them, and it was said that they awaited His advent upon the night before Easter. "The Jewish tradition," wrote Jerome, "is that Christ will come in the middle of the night, and that it will be as upon that first Easter in Egypt when the avenging angel appeared, and when the Lord passed over the dwellings of Israel and their doors were consecrated by the blood of the lamb." I believe he added, no doubt drawing his impression from Lactantius, "that the Apostolic custom which upon Easter Eve forbids the dismissal of the people before midnight, because until that hour they await the coming of Christ, owes its derivation to this. ." [2]

Jerome has told us that in the Eastern Churches it was habitual, before reading the Gospel, to light the lamps even in broad daylight (jam sole rutilante) as a sign of joy.[3] He has also frequently described the modest pomp of the Christian funerals.

Ecclesiastical discipline maintains the idea, and upon certain days and under certain forms imposes

[1] Matthew xxiv. 20.
[2] Commentator in Matt. Lib. iv., cap. xxv.
[3] Contra Vigilantium. Lib. 7.

the practice not only of prayer, but also penance. Jerome, affirming the traditional usage of the Church and at the same time rejecting the exaggerated severity of the Montanists, wrote: "We, according to the traditions of the apostles, have but one Lent, a Lent which is observed by the whole world; but they, (meaning the Montanists) observe three every year, as if three Saviours had suffered for us. Not that it is not permissible to fast the whole year through, except during the fifty days after Easter, but it is one thing to make one's offering because of a compelling law, and quite another to be actuated thereto by a voluntary impulse."[1] Although Jerome enjoined fasting upon others, and practised it himself with an austerity which would seem to us extreme, he discarded from it all subtleties and eccentricities.[2] He reminds us that fasting and prayer, in short the most holy deeds, are fruitless when they are not accompanied by or are not a preparation to conversion; to presume to move God by our vows and sacrifices whilst persevering in sin is a form of mental blindness.[3] None have valued the practice of evangelical councils more highly than did Jerome, and none have more forcibly reminded those who freely bound themselves to the observance of them, of the duty of steadfast faithfulness. He attests the great law of clerical continence which was so early imposed by the Church upon her ministers, and

[1] Ep. xli. ad Marcellum 3.
[2] Ep. lii. ad Nepotianum Presbyterum 12.
[3] Commentar. in Jeremiah, prophetam. Lib. iii., cap. xiv.

which, through the invincible constancy of the Popes, has prevailed for the greater glory of God, as well as for the greater good of souls. "What," asked Jerome of Vigilantius, who wished to do away with this holy law, "what will become of the Eastern Churches, of the Churches of Egypt, and of the Apostolic See, none of which raise to holy orders any but those who have never lost their chastity, those who abide in continence, or those husbands who consent to abandon their marital rights?"[1]

The practice of evangelical counsels took root, so to speak, in monasticism, in which it found a firm and lasting organisation. We already know how the historian of St Paul the hermit, of St Malchus, and of St Hilarion, recorded the early history of this life in the East. In the West, in Rome, he was the spiritual director of the noble souls who aspired to the life of the desert, and who even in the midst of the world were able to create for themselves a solitude. Through him we know every detail of those stern existences in which ceaseless sacrifice reigned supreme. Chastity, poverty and obedience, have ever found in Jerome the most sincere and eloquent of panegyrists, but he never thought that these exalted virtues replaced all others; he believed and taught that they should be quickened by a virtue still more excellent in which they culminate, namely charity.

The recluse whose lips gave utterance to so many harsh sayings was moved to gentleness when he

[1] Contra Vigilantium. Lib. 2.

THE DOCTRINE OF SAINT JEROME

glorified this supreme virtue which seeks and loves God before all else, and which in God seeks and loves its neighbour, who was created and redeemed by the eternal love. In his efforts to win the souls of men to the exercise of charity, he extolled, one might almost say that he exaggerated, the facility of practising it. "Fasting exhausts the body," he said, "vigils mortify the flesh, and alms are costly. . . No matter how ardent the faith, blood is not shed in martyrdom without anguish and horror, and yet many have done these things; charity alone is easy to practise.   But the possession of this virtue is, however, rare. Who, following Paul's example, is willing to be accursed for his fellow-men? Who weeps with those who weep and rejoices with those who rejoice, who suffers through another's sorrow?"[1]

And again we find this passage: "To give one's life for one's fellow-men, to fight against sin even to the shedding of blood, is to walk in charity and to imitate Jesus Christ who loved us enough to suffer the anguish of the cross for our salvation."[2]

These were the sentiments expressed by Jerome upon the subject of tasks which are ordained by God and imposed upon us by the Church, but which receive from charity alone the supreme and finishing touch. Is it astonishing that he should have spoken in the same way of a task of which the Church, no doubt, approves, but which it has never generally prescribed? Jerome was a born explorer, and both

---

[1] Commentar. in Epist. ad Galatas.   Lib. iii., cap. v. 14.
[2] Commentar. in Epist. ad Ephesios.   Lib. iii.

his nature and his devout spirit predisposed him to the pilgrimages of which he has left us an undying example, and of which he has shown the way to so many. He lived in the times when pilgrims were drawn to Palestine by a pious longing to find again the traces of our Lord's footsteps—when Silvia of Aquitaine made a journey to the Holy Land, and left us in the *Peregrinatio* a programme of liturgical festival which the Abbé Duchesne has aptly named "The Religious Week in Jerusalem in the fourth century."[1] Jerome, however, did not consider these pious journeys to be essential or imperative; he even deterred his friend Paulinus from making a pilgrimage to Palestine. "It is not the mere fact of having seen Jerusalem," he wrote him, "but the fact of having long dwelt there, which is laudable. The city worthy of our longings and of our praise is not that which slew the prophets and shed the blood of Christ, it is the city situated upon a mountain, exposed to the gaze of all, at whose base flow the waters of a river, the city which the apostle declares to be the mother of the saints, and in which he rejoices at possessing rights of citizenship with the just.

In speaking thus, I do not convince myself of inconstancy, I do not condemn my conduct. Like Abraham, I have abandoned my kindred and my fatherland, and I do not pretend that I acted in vain; but I dare not restrict God's omnipotence within narrow limits, I dare not imprison in a corner of this earth, Him whom the heavens cannot contain.

[1] Abbé Duchesne.

Believers are judged not according to the various places which they inhabit, but according to the merit of their faith. True worshippers do not worship the Father either at Jerusalem or upon Mt. Garizim; for God is spirit, and it is in spirit and in truth that He should be adored. . The spot where stood the cross, the spot where our Lord rose again, benefit those only who carry their cross, who daily rise again with Jesus Christ, and who show themselves worthy of dwelling amid these sacred places.

The kingdom of heaven is free to those who come from Jerusalem or to those who come from Britain; *the kingdom of God is indeed within us.* Anthony and all those hosts of hermits who lived in Egypt, Mesopotamia, Pontus, Cappadocia, and Armenia, never saw Jerusalem, and yet though they never set eyes upon the holy city, the gates of Paradise were opened to them. The blessed Hilarion, who was born and had lived in Palestine, went but once to Jerusalem and stayed there but one day, thus showing that he revered the sacred places which were so near to him, but that at the same time he feared to seem to restrict the Lord to one place."[1]

Seven centuries later Bernard, the ardent promoter of the second crusade, the man who almost depopulated Europe in order to send innumerable pilgrims to Asia to conquer the Holy Sepulchre, spoke in much the same words as Jerome: "A monk should strive to reach not the terrestrial but the Celestial Jerusalem." And in a charming letter

[1] Epist. lviii. ad Paulinum, 2, 3.

to the bishop of Lincoln he depicts to us an English pilgrim who had started for the holy land, but had stopped at Clairvaux and had found there the peace and the joy which he expected to taste only in Jerusalem. The whole Catholic tradition teaches us the same thing; it glorifies the good works accomplished for God and with the help of God, but it maintains a hierarchy amongst them by subjecting them all to the quickening and vivifying spirit of charity.

Such is the doctrine set forth by Jerome's works, in which we find the dogmas which a tradition of nineteen centuries has taught us to venerate and to profess. Upon several points, in accordance with the law of progress which was foreseen by Petau in the seventeenth century, and which in our own times Newman has so brilliantly illustrated, the Catholic teachings have become more definite, they have developed like the germ which grows into a tree, but they have not countenanced and will never countenance any variation which would alter and pervert a doctrine. In St Jerome the Church has recognised one of the most dependable and steadfast champions of the truth, and it has acknowledged his services and awarded him a glorious tribute, by crowning him with the aureole of a Doctor.